MANIFEST LIKE A MOTHER

How to Attract the Life You Want in the Time You Have

Francesca Amber

RIDER

RIDER

UK | USA | Canada | Ireland | Australia
India | New Zealand | South Africa

Rider is part of the Penguin Random House group of companies
whose addresses can be found at global.penguinrandomhouse.com

Penguin Random House UK
One Embassy Gardens, 8 Viaduct Gardens, London SW11 7BW

penguin.co.uk
global.penguinrandomhouse.com

First published by Rider in 2025

1

Typeset in 9.5/15 Century Gothic Pro by Six Red Marbles UK, Thetford, Norfolk
Printed and bound in India by Thomson Press India Ltd.

The authorised representative in the EEA is Penguin Random House Ireland,
Morrison Chambers, 32 Nassau Street, Dublin D02 YH68

A CIP catalogue record for this book is available from the British Library

ISBN 9781846048654

MIX
Paper | Supporting
responsible forestry
FSC
www.fsc.org   FSC® C018179

Penguin Random House is committed to a sustainable future
for our business, our readers and our planet. This book is made
from Forest Stewardship Council® certified paper.

For my daughters, Bohemia, Riva and Laveau.

For my own mother, Cassandra.

And for every mother deciding to consciously create a beautiful life for themselves and their children.

Contents

WELCOME, BITCHES

'Hi, I'm Francesca and I'm a powerful manifestor. And, guess what? So are you.'

When I first pitched this book to my publishers, they responded with, 'Why manifesting for mothers? What a goddamn niche. What makes us different and why can't we manifest and create a life of our dreams like anybody else?' Well, you only need to be a mother for a single day to know that we modern mothers are the most time- and energy-poor demographic in our society *by a mile*!

I have completely transformed my life in the last few years using the law of attraction and all kinds of strategies, which you'll find in the pages of this book. Now, I know that lots of people have used manifestation to change their lives, but the difference for me was that I did it from the depths of the trenches of motherhood. And not just motherhood, but single, Covid-19-lockdown, no-income, isolated-and-alone, gave-birth-to-*twins* and suffering-from-postnatal-depression motherhood. But more on that later.

About four years ago, when I started hosting my self-development book club, I remember picking up a popular manifesting book all about creating a powerful morning routine with great excitement and anticipation that *this* was going to change my life. I had experimented with waking up super early in the past – riding high on the coat-tails of transatlantic jet lag or during a stint of good sleeping habits or sobriety – and I was excited to try it again as I *knew* what amazing results it could garner. As I turned the pages and read that I would be required to wake up at around 5am and have the first hour of the day to myself to meditate, journal, read and exercise, I quickly realised with frustration that this was no longer going to work for me and the newborn motherhood stage of life I was in at the time.

My life back then was broken up into two-hourly cycles that ran twenty-four hours a day. Those two-hourly cycles were me breastfeeding for about twenty minutes, followed by being nap-trapped, then changing nappies, only for it to start again. Oh, and looking after my four-year-old too (or was she looking after me?).

So many self-development books have been written by well-meaning men who seem to have very little to do with the daily raising of their children. The chances of me getting to meditate while my school-age daughter tries to tell me all about her dreams from the night before were slim to none.

A short while later, I was recording a podcast with a wonderful manifesting coach and I asked her what the secret to her success was: what did she do every day by way of rituals that ensured she was on the right track to success and abundance? She informed me that her daily manifesting rituals had changed and reduced dramatically since she got a dog. A *dog!* As I sat there with a baby on each boob and a four-year-old raiding the kitchen cupboards in the background, I could scarcely believe my ears. That's when it hit me square in the tits: here I am as a woman in the deepest, darkest trenches of motherhood, trying to create my dream life using a template that people with far more time, space and energy for themselves had created. It was *never* going to work. Or, in the words of 50 Cent, I could 'die trying'.

Yes, Molly-Mae was right when she said we all have the same twenty-four hours in the day, but a day without six wake-up calls in the night, round-the-clock breastfeeding, school runs, toddler groups, laundry and making dinner *every single day* has a hell of a lot more time, space and energy in it for you to focus on your goals and dreams.

That podcast, that episode and that conversation was a transformative moment for me. I realised what my calling was: to make all this incredible work that I *know* can change people's lives possible for mothers like me.

I experienced a total life breakdown (or what I've since rebranded as a breakthrough) in 2020 with a simultaneous move across the country, a relationship break-up, the loss of my business and income, the loss of freedom (hello lockdown!) and the discovery that I was pregnant . . . with twins! I found myself going from being a happy-go-lucky single mum living in London, taking rooftop breakfasts around the pool with my eldest daughter at Shoreditch House, relishing my child-free time in the big city with friends, treating Tinder like it was Amazon same-day delivery for men and working on my salon empire, to being isolated for months on end with only my toddler for company.

We lived in a cramped, outdated house which an old lady had recently died in (RIP, but her taste in brown carpets which I couldn't afford to replace was *hideous*) in a quiet countryside village where I hardly knew anybody. My business was closed for the foreseeable and my income as a self-employed queen was *gone*. My twin pregnancy weighed heavily on me as I struggled with depression, to be blamed equally on hormones and my new circumstances. As all that I knew and loved about my life fell away at an alarming rate, one thing remained and always will: the ability at any point to remember that I am a powerful creator; that I can take control, change my mindset and manifest the life I want to live. I guess there's no better place to start than at the bottom, standing among the wreckage of my previous life.

I started my law of attraction podcast initially as something to do after one 'isolation creation' too many, painting my entire kitchen *pink*! The podcast gave me a focus and served to distract me from the living hell of eternal lockdown in quarantine. It soon became a lifeline, something that not only saved me but enabled me to *thrive*, creating a far better life for myself than I ever thought possible.

The good news is this: I did it! I took the tatters of my life and created something incredible using my mindset alone. I did it. I did it with tiny newborn twins and a toddler in tow. I did it on my own. I did it with no money. I did it with no partner to help. I did it with no coaches or courses or retreats – and so can you!

As I sit here and write this, reflecting back on what my life was like then, I can scarcely recognise it from the life I live today. Yes, I have manifested more money than I could have ever dreamed of earning and all the trappings that a basic bitch like me would want: family trips to Barbados, a dream house with big gates, a Pinterest-perfect kitchen and a designer vagina, but it's so much more than the material stuff. I now have an exciting, fulfilling career as a podcaster and now *author* (hey!) and a life filled with beautiful people, stimulating friendships, fun events, adventures, travel and love. It genuinely feels as good as it looks.

I know that you are picking up this book hoping there is finally a way to dedicate some time to creating the life you want. This is despite all the commitments and responsibilities that take away so much of your energy. And yes, in a way, being a mother and all the ways that society is not set up for us to thrive makes it harder, I admit that – but, in another sense, it makes it so much easier too.

Ask any mother what their priority is in life and almost every single one will say, 'My children'. Well, the great news is that by taking the time and energy to work on yourself, on your mindset, on your goals and creating the life of your dreams, not only are you doing it for you, but you are also doing it for your children. We all know what it's like to parent with an empty cup. When we're tired, burnt out, haven't socialised, haven't rested, haven't had a change of scenery – when we lose ourselves and our direction, abandon our passions, neglect our relationships and fail in our self-care efforts – we become a shell of our former selves. The scary thing is that it happens slowly . . . it happens insidiously. It begins the second you give birth and all the care and attention on you and your well-being is immediately transferred to your new, tiny human. It begins when we are expected to relentlessly put our babies before ourselves from now until the day we die. It begins when we absorb the invisible load. It's become so normal to take care of everyone else's needs before our own that it's an almost alien concept to ask ourselves, 'Am I living the life that I want?', 'What do I truly desire?' and 'What are my goals?'

The best gift you can give to your family is a healthy, healed, happy version of you. I wrote that line and deleted it three times, because although this is important and true, I don't want you to do this just for your children. I want you to do this for YOU.

This book is about manifestation but it's also about strategy. Because it's all well and good knowing *what* to do, but if you're too damn tired or overwhelmed to do it . . . well, that's no good.

This is important because in this season of your life, you are going to be busier than at any other time. You are going to have more expectations and more responsibilities placed on you by your family, friends, work and society than ever before. If you aren't careful, there will be no time, space or energy left for you to cook up what *you* truly want, and nothing tastes worse than regret. That is why strategy is so important. You want to run your home, your family and your business, but also leave space for *you*.

If this is feeling uncomfortable or selfish, know this: we often talk about giving our children all the things we didn't have in our own childhood, but why when we say this do we mean material items – maybe the must-have designer shoes of the season or the gaming console that everyone has? When you work on your own personal development, build love and trust with yourself to create a life of your dreams, you give your children so much more. You give them the gifts of witnessing you upholding standards and boundaries, enjoying emotional regulation, living with healthy habits and modelling beautiful relationships. What more could you possibly want to give them?

This book is unlike any other manifesting book you've read. I'm not going to tell you to meditate each day and journal when you wake up because, frankly, what mum has time for that? Instead, this book will explore different ways you can incorporate manifesting into your everyday life – hacking your way to more energy using your menstrual cycle, allowing your home to be your ally in reaching your goals, turning your endless list of jobs into self-care rituals, dressing for the life you want, and so much more. I promise, it's not going to add to your plate, but simply rearrange it to make space for the life you want to create.

Before we dive into manifesting like the magnetic, multitasking, miracle-making mothers we are, let's start at the beginning. I'm going to kick things off with the basic theory of the law of attraction – not because I think you've never heard of it (I'm assuming you're as obsessed as me), but because even us seasoned manifesting veterans sometimes need reminding. The basics are called the basics for a reason – they're the foundation. And if your foundation's feeling a bit wobbly under the weight of school runs, laundry mountains and forgotten PE kits, then it's time to dust it off and realign. Let's go back to where the magic starts.

Chapter 1

THE LAW OF ATTRACTION

'The law of attraction at a very basic bitch level is a bit like ordering from Amazon, except Amazon is the Universe.'

I first discovered the law of attraction in my early twenties. I found it the way any mid-noughties girl did and that was through the iconic book *The Secret*. I was introduced to it by my friend Grace. I turned the pages in disbelief, faster and faster like that boy in *The NeverEnding Story*. I read every single word, slammed the book shut and declared, 'This is going to *change my life*!' And, spoiler alert, it did.

The law of attraction at a very basic bitch level is a bit like ordering from Amazon, except Amazon is the Universe. You can order whatever you want from the Universe at any time; whether it's a physical item, an amount of money, an experience, an outcome to a situation, a person or a feeling – *anything*! Here's the scary part: it's working *all – the – time*, whether you like it or not!

I know that manifesting has its sceptics, naysayers and outright disbelievers – and I can understand why. Those who have spent their lives in struggle will absolutely resist the idea that they can create their own reality. However, there are so many forces or real, physical things that we are unable to sense, but they're there regardless and we have no problem in believing in them. Think about the invisible force of gravity which is holding us down, how a dog can hear a pitch of a whistle that is undetectable to our ears or how Wi-Fi is all around us, connecting us to each other. We can't see these invisible forces, but they are there nonetheless, just like the invisible energies that surround us.

Time and time again, it's been proven that everything, yes *everything*, is simply energy which is vibrating at different frequencies and, when frequencies match, they tune in and connect, much like a radio.

Actually, let's think of a radio. It works by tuning in to specific frequencies of electromagnetic waves. Radio stations broadcast their music or shows on different frequencies. When you turn the dial on a radio, you're selecting a specific frequency and, once the radio is tuned to that station's frequency, you can hear it clearly. If you're not on the exact frequency, all you get is static.

The law of attraction works in a similar way, but instead of a radio, *you* are the 'receiver'. Your thoughts, emotions and energy emit their own 'frequency'. When you focus on positive thoughts, gratitude and the life you desire, you tune yourself to the frequency of those things, like tuning into a radio station.

When you're aligned with that frequency, you start to 'receive' similar energy in return – opportunities, ideas and situations that match what you're broadcasting. If you're focused on worry or negativity, it's like being off the station's frequency – you won't get the results you want.

The fact is, most people spend their lives thinking more about what they don't want than what they do. A very simple rule is to give attention to what you want to manifest into your reality. Each time you catch yourself dwelling on what you *don't* want, refocus and give your energy to what you do want.

We Don't Attract What We Want, We Attract What We Are

The core principle of the law of attraction is that like attracts like. Basically, whatever energy you're putting out there, you're going to attract right back to you.

Now, this is where rookies will say, 'OK, I want to win the lottery and go on a date with Eddie Hearn.' (Is that just my weird crush? OK.) Then they are surprised when it doesn't manifest. Why doesn't it work? Well, it's not as simple as order it and it arrives. In order to *receive* what we desire, we must first believe we are truly able to receive it and also become the kind of person who would receive it. That's where so much of 'the work' comes in. We must begin the task of working on our past traumas and the resulting limiting beliefs that are holding us back. I will give you an example from the one long manifestation experiment that is my life.

I grew up with a mum, dad and older sister. My dad was fun at times and had lots of great qualities, but he was quite an intense person who made many choices I would never repeat with my own children. When I was around 11, my parents got divorced and Dad moved out, and I felt a lightness I'd never experienced before. My mum, my sister and I got so much closer, I was finally allowed a hamster (win!) and my mum suddenly had a big circle of single mum friends – life felt like a party. This lasted a year or two until my mum met her new partner, aka exactly the same as my dad but with a different face. He was often aggressive, bigoted and angry. I moved out as soon as I could to the bright lights and safety of London, which I loved and which gave me the safety and security I craved.

As an adult, almost twenty years later, I sit here as a single woman with three daughters, living alone, financially independent, emotionally hyper-independent and reluctant to date. I have managed to manifest so many incredible things in my life including wealth, success, amazing friendships, exciting experiences and so much more – but still I'm single. Why? Because the role men have played in the story of my life has been such a strong narrative that 'men are bad' and 'women thrive on their own' that it takes A LOT to work through that. Is it impossible? No. Is it my priority? Also no. I've been too busy being a boss bitch, making a number-one podcast, raising my daughters, writing a book and living my best life!

I'm not mad at myself that I haven't taken the time and energy to fully work on my love-limiting beliefs, rather I'm proud of myself for recognising how my narrative is shaping my life. Yes, we totally *can* change any and every aspect of our lives, but it truly does take some intentional time and energy to resolve. Time this mama just hasn't had . . . *yet*!

When it comes down to it, we don't simply attract what we want, we attract what we are. That's where so many different techniques and strategies, such as cyclical living, visualisation, gratitude, emotional freedom technique (EFT), dressing for the life you want, aligned action and setting your environment up for success, come in to elevate your standards, ways of living and habits until you *become* what you are aiming to magnetise into your life. We're going to explore these techniques, which I've specifically curated for those in their motherhood era, a little further into the book. One promise I want to reiterate here is that this isn't going to be just another manifesting book telling you to journal and meditate each morning. I don't know how your motherhood's going and what your mornings look like, but if they're anything like mine, we don't have the time for that!

Now, before you go thinking this is all just 'positive vibes' with no backbone, there's actually some fascinating science to back it up. Dr James R. Doty, a Stanford neurosurgeon, suggests that practices associated with manifestation, such as writing down intentions, vocalising them and visualising success, can engage the brain's default mode network (DMN). This network is involved in introspection and self-referential thinking, and by repeatedly focusing on specific goals, individuals may enhance neural pathways related to these objectives, potentially increasing the likelihood of achieving them. Doty emphasises that this process is grounded in neuroscience rather than mystical thinking.

Our brains are constantly scanning the environment and zeroing in on what we focus on most – a concept called the reticular activating system (or RAS, for short). This small bunch of nerves at the base of our brainstem is our personal search engine, always finding evidence to support our beliefs and expectations. So, when you consciously direct your focus towards your goals or desires, the RAS begins to filter your world, showing you more of the things that align with those thoughts. It's like when you start thinking about buying a certain type of car. You begin to see them *everywhere*! Did an abundance of these cars suddenly materialise out of nowhere? Of course not. You are now seeing what was always there. The law of attraction taps right into this system, training your mind to notice opportunities, connections and solutions that were probably there all along but now shine in neon!

How to Manifest

The law of attraction isn't just passive daydreaming and hoping. It's about taking inspired action and aligning your mindset with what you're calling in. Imagine wanting to manifest your dream job while sitting on the sofa thinking, 'One day . . .' Nothing's going to change until you get up and send that email, take that course or network with those people in your field. Manifestation is about more than just wishing; it's about believing in what's possible, feeling grateful before it arrives and moving in sync with what you desire. When you combine a positive mindset with real action, you're sending a powerful signal to the Universe that says, 'I'm ready.' And when you're ready, the Universe starts working with you.

I find the best way to manifest something into my life is to follow these five steps:

Step one: Gratitude

Before we ask for *anything*, we should first find gratitude for all that we already have. If the area of your life you're looking to transform is pretty shitty to start with, it needs even *more* gratitude! It sounds pretty basic, but intentional gratitude can seriously change your life.

For example, if you want to attract higher vibe friendships but are surrounded by unaligned, maybe even toxic friends, you must *still* show gratitude for them while recognising they are no longer for you. It may be that you can say thank you to those friends for showing you want you *don't* want in your future friendships.

It can be tempting to skip straight to what we want in the future, but if we stop for a moment and truly give thanks for all that we have, the Universe has no choice but to deliver more to be thankful for. Remember, what you focus on grows, and there is good and bad in *every* person, situation, city, job or relationship. Therefore, by showing gratitude for what we already have, we aren't asking for more of the same status quo, but rather more of the good parts.

Step two: Decide

Get clear and decide what you want. The more specific your goal, the more specific your results will be. So many of us go about our lives complaining that we aren't living how we want, but not being clear on what it is that we *do* want.

An easy way to make sure you are being specific enough is to set SMART goals, a framework introduced by George Doran in 1981. A SMART goal is Specific, Measurable, Achievable, Relevant and Time-bound.

Let's take me writing this book as an example. This was a fucking miracle if I'm honest. I'm a single mum who carries the entire invisible load of a family of four, two of my children are preschoolers (if you know, you know), I'm not officially diagnosed with attention deficit hyperactivity disorder (ADHD), but there's definitely something going on there, and I am the sole breadwinner for my family. The chances of me not writing this book were *huge*!

Anyway, if I'd simply said, 'I want to write a book in 2025', it would *neverrrrr* have happened! However, as soon as I made it a SMART goal, it was almost as good as done. Here's how to make your goal SMART:

- **S**pecific: Clearly define the goal. Avoid vague or general statements.
  Example: Instead of 'I want to write a book,' say, 'I will write a 60,000-word book by March 2025.'
- **M**easurable: Make the goal quantifiable so you can track progress. Remember, what gets measured, gets improved.
  Example: 'I will write 2,000 words per week.'

- **A**chievable: Set a goal that is challenging but realistic, given your resources and constraints.
  Example: Writing for two and a half hours twice a week instead of every day if you're single-handedly raising three children some days with no break or help.
- **R**elevant: Align the goal with your larger purpose or priorities.
  Example: Writing the book aligns with your passion for sharing knowledge about manifestation and supporting mothers.
- **T**ime-bound: Set a deadline to create urgency and focus.
  Example: 'I will finish the first draft by 1 March 2025.'

I would love for you to think about one particular goal you have, something you are 100 per cent sure you want, and apply this SMART framework to it. It's fun learning new shit, but it's even better to implement it immediately!

Step three: Believe

Belief is the hardest step for many as this is where a lot of the 'undoing' or 'unlearning' work comes in. In order to truly believe, we must dispel long-held beliefs about ourselves, others and the world around us. This is totally possible through all kinds of self-development work and self-help techniques, some of which we'll cover in the chapters that follow, and others that are far too complex to go into within the remit of this book. The degree to which you discover and demolish your limiting beliefs will directly correlate to the degree you are able to manifest.

Step four: Action

You can't spell the law of attraction without action. Believe your desire is on its way and *act* accordingly. Belief, you see, isn't just about thoughts, but actions too. I find the Universe always speeds up my manifestation, almost supercharges it, when I take aligned action. Physically moving and making something happen with pure intention is one of my secret weapons.

When I wanted to marry a guy I hadn't even been on a first date with yet, I symbolically decluttered my little one-bedroom flat in London to make space for him to be there. We got engaged six months later.

When I was trying to get pregnant with my first child who I really wanted to be a daughter, I went to Oxford Street and bought a highly symbolic item – a little pink sleepsuit with bows all over it. That became the first outfit she wore, and her name was Bo!

If I truly believed I was going to get my dream job in Paris after watching one too many episodes of *Emily in Paris*, I would intentionally declutter my home so that I could easily pack up and go. I would also start French lessons. The action part is super important. What action can you take *now* towards your goal?

Step five: Receive

You would think that the final step of the process, 'receive', would be a no-brainer, but sometimes this is the hardest one of all. Now that you have shown thanks, decided, believed and taken action, you must also let go and just allow yourself to receive. I always think that manifesting is a perfect, delicate mix of science and art. There is a fine line to be danced between manically manifesting and sitting back and waiting for it to fall into your lap.

So, how do you receive? Be open to opportunities, take inspired action and be receptive to your manifestation coming through in a way you never expected – be flexible and curious. To truly receive, you must feel worthy of what you desire. To feel worthy, ask yourself daily, 'Am I living the life of a person who would receive this kind of manifestation?' If your goal is to become the most successful businesswoman in your hood, but you get up late, are never organised and slack off with simple tasks all the time, it's unlikely you believe that you can achieve that with your current day-to-day life.

Something I love about this concept and spending time on your self-development is that you can completely transform your daily life and habits, one small step at a time. And, over time, this will give you a whole new identity and belief system. This book is going to show you how – through elevating your existence via your environment, your daily routine and the standards you set for yourself. Get excited!

I'm forty at the time of writing and not only have I managed to work for myself for over ten years, but I've purchased and renovated three properties by myself, been a single mother to three children, been through a divorce and built an incredible brand which saved me, all from nothing. I don't say that to be Braggy-Sue, but it's the daily actions that have led to me taking bigger and bigger bets on creating a beautiful life for me and my children.

Can you imagine how much love and respect I have for myself now? I love myself because I can always rely on myself to find a solution when times get tough. I love myself because I will put in the effort and energy to support my family and I love myself because I am always looking to curate the most beautiful life for myself. I'm literally my own best friend or, in the words of Cher, 'Mom, I *am* a rich man!'

Anyway, I got sidetracked there. Back to receiving. This is where we must align our energy with the frequency we wish to attract. Take action and speak and think in alignment with your goal. For example, if you were manifesting your dream relocation to LA you wouldn't sign a new three-year lease on a house in the UK. Ya know?

When it comes to the elusive 'letting go', this is the trickiest of mental tightropes to walk. It's such a head fuck at the beginning, but I swear it becomes easier. The more you consciously create your life and work with the Universe, the more you will learn to trust it.

Remember being heartbroken over your high-school sweetheart who cheated three times in the same month? Remember being fired from that toxic job that was leading nowhere? Often (if not *always*), we look back and think, 'Thank fuck – I dodged a bullet there.' As we recognise this, we get to surrender as maybe we don't always know best. The great news is, you're not doing this all alone. This is where co-creation comes in.

A note on co-creation

For years and years, I was what I now know to be a 'controlling manifestor' and I was damn good at it! Ever since I picked up *The Secret* and discovered what manifesting and cosmic ordering was, I would set extremely specific goals – and I would achieve them. That's kind of how me sharing the law of attraction first began to take off as people *loved* hearing about my incredibly specific manifestation stories.

I took full responsibility (and credit!) for the manifestations, but it was also quite stressful. What if what you're trying to manifest is not the right thing? Worse still, what if it doesn't happen? This is where co-creation comes in. Whenever we are manifesting, we aren't doing it alone – we are co-creating with a higher power. Now, what does that actually mean? Is it God, God-dess, Jesus, Allah, the Universe? I don't know, but it's a loving, powerful energy that, over time, I have learnt to communicate with and trust. By the way, I was today years old when I found out what I am, religiously speaking. It's slightly embarrassing that I learnt this from a 25-year-old on Tinder, but, hey, we learn where we can. I'm totally an agnostic. I'm not an atheist – what, there's nothing *at all* out there? Nah. I don't subscribe to that. But I am a huge believer that whatever *it* is, we cannot even comprehend. How can we say something so vast, so complex, so *unhuman* is a race, a man, a brunette? Isn't that wild?

So, we don't know what this presence is, nor do we know if it's a human, a Gemini or a Chihuahua – we know none of this, but is also doesn't matter; all that matters is that we learn to co-create with it. Maybe you already have an idea of what it is to you? Christians call it God, Muslims call it Allah, Pagans call it Gaia, the ancient Romans called it Jupiter. Truly, who the fuck knows, but can we all agree we feel a force and it is loving and powerful?

When I manifest now, rather than setting an extremely fixed goal, I ask for 'this or something better', trusting that the Universe sometimes has a better path planned out for me than I could have ever imagined. I also let go of some (read *some*, not *all*!) of the action and ask the Universe to show me the way. There is something very liberating about the fact that it's not *all* up to us.

I think back to the pandemic and how if I had manifested what I wanted back then, my life would be totally different now. I had a beauty salon in London which I was so proud of, but the working environment had turned a bit toxic and I had just bought my second home in the countryside to raise my daughter nearer to my family and further away from daily knife crime. When I found out I was pregnant, my plan was to take my new baby (I didn't realise there were two at this point!) down to London for a couple of days a week, work in my old salon all the hours I could while I was there, relying on my then kinda partner to care for the baby during that time, and then spend the rest of the time at home in the countryside with my girls. Perfect! One by one, blocks to that plan started to pop up.

Firstly, I was unknowingly carrying a litter, like an alley cat (I'm adventurous, but trying to carry twin babies and a suitcase on a train every week wasn't for me).

Next, my ex and I couldn't agree a plan for who would have our daughters when, so I had no child-free days to work.

Then, my salon shut down along with the rest of the beauty industry.

Every nail in the coffin of that old plan frustrated me more and more. Why was the Universe, which had always been so good to me, now against me?! What I didn't know back then is that it was working very much in my favour. Had just one aspect of that situation worked out, I probably would have pushed and struggled to make that highly fragile and completely unsustainable shit show work for years. Instead, I was forced to let go of everything I had planned and knew to start completely afresh. The Universe gave me an abundance of time, energy and space as well as a life I hated to motivate and inspire me to start a podcast, to help not only my mental health and shitty life situation, but so many other people's too.

The rest is history, of course. My money problems disappeared, I could work from home around my young daughters and life became *epic*, hosting events, buying my dream home, walking red carpets and getting book deals! So, sometimes when everything feels like it's falling apart, it is in fact falling *together* to create something wilder than you could have ever imagined.

The fantastic thing about the law of attraction is that *anyone* can do it and it works for *anything*. You don't have to stop reading if you don't want to be rich, if you don't want to run your own business or if you don't want to write a book. Everyone's idea of success is their own and you have the power to create whatever life you desire.

Now you know how the law of attraction works and that it's entirely possible to manifest the life of your dreams, what could possibly hold you back? Often, it's not a lack of belief or effort, but the reality of the season you're in. This book is for mothers in the trenches of motherhood, navigating the chaos of sleepless nights, endless snack requests and the ever-growing to-do list. It's easy to feel like your dreams are on pause, that manifesting is something for another version of you – one who isn't so exhausted. But the truth is, your power to create your dream life isn't waiting for a more perfect season. It's right here, in the midst of this one. So, how do you embrace where you are while still stepping into everything you want? Let's dive in to the next chapter.

Chapter 2

YOUR MOTHERHOOD ERA

'Appreciate what season of your life you currently find yourself in and be gentle with yourself.'

As you begin to embrace the idea that you are the powerful creator of your own reality, the architect of your life, the curator of your dreams, I just want to add a little side note with this chapter about respecting the season of your life. As you discover just how powerful you are, you may also simultaneously be the most tired, overwhelmed and burnt out you've ever been.

As mothers, we dedicate so much of our time and energy in service of others. In years gone by, as we entered the motherhood era of our lives, we would have been traditionally supported by many other women within our tribe: our mother, aunties, sisters and friends. There's a reason they say 'It takes a village to raise a child.' (Does anyone know where to find this village? I'm asking for a friend.)

Motherhood today can often feel like such an overwhelming, isolating journey. In the past, mothers were deeply embedded within their communities or tribes, surrounded by a collective support system. This network shared the responsibilities of child-rearing, offering physical help, emotional support and wisdom passed down through the generations. Am I the only one who daydreams of setting up a commune with my friends or sees a Mormon with several wives who all share duties and think – that looks *lovely*!? So long as there are no threesomes and I get a night off from childcare and house-work a week, I'm down for some sister wives!

According to my all-time favourite book which has trans-formed the way I mother my girls, *The Continuum Concept* by Jean Liedloff, these traditional tribes and societies understood the value of communal care. Babies were rarely out of a care-giver's arms, and children were raised not just by their parents, but by an entire community. Mothers didn't bear the brunt of parenting alone – we were supported, respected and guided by others who shared in our joys and also our burdens.

In stark contrast, modern mothers are often left to navi-gate the immense demands of raising children in near-total daily isolation. The pressures of managing a household, working and parenting fall squarely on our shoulders, with little external support. Societal structures have shifted away from collective living, and many mothers live far from family or lack access to affordable childcare. Add to this the expectation of perfection perpetuated by social media, and it's no wonder many mothers feel like they're failing despite giving their all. This isolation is not just unnatural, it's also unsustainable. It leaves us mothers depleted, emotionally and physically, with little time or energy for ourselves. Reconnecting with the concept of community – even if it's creating a modern 'tribe' of friends, neighbours or other mothers – can be a lifeline, reminding us that motherhood was never meant to be a solo endeavour.

As I mentioned in the Introduction, so many traditional law of attraction books were written by men who don't even *mention* childcare as a fact of everyday life and so, as you read through this book, I want you to appreciate what season of your life you currently find yourself in and be gentle with yourself.

Matrescence

Have you heard of the word matrescence? Incredibly, I only discovered it when it was brought to my attention by one of my dear podcast listeners (they always tell me the best shit!) – annoyingly, *after* I had given birth to all three of my daughters. As with so many aspects of being a woman that I discover later in life, I cannot believe we aren't taught this in school.

Matrescence is the process of becoming a mother, encompassing the physical, emotional, psychological and social transformations that occur as a woman transitions from maidenhood into motherhood. The term was created by anthropologist Dana Raphael with lots of parallels drawn with adolescence, as both involve profound identity shifts and hormonal changes (i.e. you're not going to know who the hell you are and why you feel the way you do . . . for quite a while).

New mothers experience so much, from physical changes such as hormone fluctuations and physical recovery from pregnancy and birth, to intense emotions, psychological changes and adjusting to changes in dynamics at work, in relationships and even in society. Matrescence acknowledges that becoming a mother is a huge developmental process which takes years, and is not a one-day event. It helps normalise the struggles many women face by reframing motherhood as a complex journey rather than something women are 'naturally' expected to handle with ease. It also highlights the need for compassion and support during this transformation. It's incredible how many women wrongly think they have postnatal depression when it's actually just a part of this huge process that every single doctor and midwife forgot to tell us about.

Remember, when a baby is born, so is a mother. This is still true if it's not your first baby. Adjusting from being a mother of one to a mother of three took me *years* to get my head around. The costs, the logistics of it all – it seemed huge to me. (I just realised I really minimised my truth there. It didn't just *seem* huge, it *was* huge.) This seems an odd time to mention this, but it's relevant. I had a little Chihuahua called Ava in my twenties and I loved her. I took her everywhere with me and I loved that she was so portable. I could just slip her in my bag and we'd sneak into any number of restaurants and shops. It was great! When she was around six, I contemplated getting her a companion, a little rescue Chihuahua with a tongue that wouldn't stay in. After a couple of days, I realised that having two dogs would be so much harder than one. I would no longer be able to simply put Ava under my arm or in my bag. It was going to be a ball-ache. That was two Chihuahuas. Can you imagine how I felt going from one to three children on my own?

This feels the right time to point out that everyone's matrescence will be different, even within their own pregnancies. When I had my first daughter, Bohemia, I was over the moon. I was married, she was an easy baby and we travelled the world with her like those annoying people you see who book a round-the-world flight with their baby in a sling. That was me! However, second time around, I was alone, we were in a lockdown, I was poor, there were now three babies fighting for my attention and *it – was – savage*. It took me a good three years to truly adjust.

The Ebb and Flow of Motherhood

What's right for somebody else in a different stage of motherhood may not be right for you. And what feels impossible for you right now may become possible in just a short few months. The nature of motherhood is that it is ever-changing, and we change with it – the demands on our time, energy and physical space ebb and flow. Ironically, as I found myself single, with newborn twins, having just lost my business and with no money, I found myself more motivated and productive than ever. That's not the case for everyone. Four years down the line and my youngest daughters are still preschoolers. I often beat myself up for not having enough time and energy for Bohemia and there are regularly days when I collapse into bed overstimulated, worn out, still in my clothes and with nothing left to give. I know I'm not the only one – we are a generation of mothers who are feeling so overwhelmed by the demands of modern life that we often don't even make the time to think about what our goals and dreams are, let alone how to reach them.

When I first became a law of attraction podcaster, I made some friends within this wellness and mindset industry, but sometimes I would find myself feeling so frustrated that those without children or who weren't the primary caregivers were able to dedicate so much of their time and energy to themselves, their businesses and creating their dream lives. It was always a comparison that was going to make me feel like shit, like I was on the back foot and that I could never catch up. I wasn't acknowledging or respecting the season of life I found myself in.

As you look at your life right now, are you perhaps experiencing any of the following?

- Suffering with a difficult pregnancy
- Recovering from a traumatic birth
- Dealing with a neurodivergent child
- Preparing to move across the country or globe
- In the trenches of newborn motherhood
- Fighting an illness which is robbing you of your joy and energy
- Have three under three at home and losing your mind

- Grieving for somebody or something
- Caring for an elderly parent
- Going through a painful divorce
- Approaching the 'empty nest' years of life

Any of these situations in our lives are going to have a profound impact upon us, our energy levels, motivation, tolerance for bullshit and desire for change. These situations or phases of our lives are also going to have a massive impact on the kind of goals we are able to set for ourselves.

For example, a concept I *love* and I know works incredibly is the idea of a very early-morning routine; a morning where you rise a good hour before the rest of your household and spend uninterrupted time journaling, meditating and working on you. Doing this is incredible and yields such great results, but, when I discovered this technique, I was co-sleeping with two breast-feeding newborns and a four-year-old. There was no way in hell I was getting out of that bed unnoticed and with my tits intact. It's a great technique, but it wasn't for me at that time. You may find that with other concepts and techniques we talk about as we go through the book. What's exciting is that, within these pages, you will find rituals and even mindset shifts that are totally doable, and if practised even semi-consistently, they will change your life.

Set goals that align with your season of life

Every New Year I host a fabulous goal-setting party with thousands of my listeners online. Each year, this process is formulated to create the life you love, one year at a time. As a part of this, one of the things I like to get crystal clear early on is, 'What is my motto or theme this year?' This theme will be my number-one priority for the year, the one thing that will help elevate every other area of my life. Often, in the day-to-day busyness of life, we can't remember our top-ten goals, but we *can* always remember our motto and it helps to keep us on point and aligned throughout the year. For each year, there may be a very different answer, and I know personally mine have always varied. Your theme could be connection, it may be adventure and fun or maybe it's health.

The first year I hosted this goal-setting party, I was deep in the newborn trenches and living under not only a UK national lockdown but also my very own personal lockdown as doing *anything* outside the house with three tiny children was incredibly hard. I could have been forgiven for thinking this wasn't a year for me to set any real goals, but what I discovered is that it was about setting the *right* kind of goals for that season of my life.

I looked at what my daily life looked like, what I could change and what I couldn't. Well, I spent every day the same way: I would wake up at around 6am, cry, feed my babies every hour for at least 15 minutes, change their nappies every couple of hours, feed me and Bohemia the best I could in between, try to keep all three children occupied with daily walks, playing, bath time and snuggling on the sofa and an exciting trip once a week to the supermarket to restock. That – was – *it*!

What could I change? Well, the babies still had their hourly feeding and changing schedule; I couldn't change that. We couldn't travel, go out to dinner, go shopping or anything other than a walk around the village and visits to family really. Therefore, despite how much I may have craved adventure, travel, fun times with friends, festivals and maybe even dating, setting those kinds of goals without recognising they didn't fit in with my current motherhood era would have left me feeling like a huge failure and more frustrated than ever. I know this first-hand as a local guy who was actually quite hot came round around eight weeks after my twins were born to help me get my Christmas tree out of my loft. He stayed for a drink afterwards and hearing how different his lockdown was to mine (he was having secret parties with childless, single friends every single week) made me feel like *shit*.

Anyway, back to the goal-setting party. Once I realised, acknowledged, accepted and even embraced the season I was in, I was then able to set goals for my life that my current circumstances would support, rather than hinder. I realised that so many things I wanted to do, places I wanted to go and experiences I wanted to have depended upon me having money. I realised that this season of my life may have felt restrictive, but it was super helpful for making me focus in on what I *needed* rather than what I wanted. I made a commitment that day to focus solely on making money. If I was going to be trapped at home for months on end, sitting on the sofa each night as my children slept with no possibility of fun or adventure, I may as well work, right? I sure wouldn't want to when the whole world opened up to me again and distracted me in a million different ways.

Focusing on just making money gave me so many gifts. It gave me the gift of time as I was able to hire a nanny to come and sit with the twins while I worked and, later on, nursery so I could have some much-needed me time. It gave me the gift of a home big enough for my growing family. It gave me the gift of travel and experiences as I took my daughters all over the world from a safari to an iconic house on a rock in the ocean in Cornwall. It gave me stability, security, safety and so much more.

Can you see now how sometimes these phases of motherhood that restrict us in so many ways can also be blessings as we redirect our energies and laser focus in on what we *can* do?

The slowing down of life when we have children can be the greatest gift if only you tap into it.

Ask yourself the following questions:

- What motherhood era do you find yourself in now?
- What restrictions do you have on your life?
- What hidden blessings could those restrictions give you?
- What one area of your life could you focus on that would raise the quality of every other area of your life too?

As you fine-tune what you are able to make space and energy for in your life, it seems the perfect time to enter the next chapter of this book, which is all about cyclical living. This the *biggest* hack for managing your energy and, Lord knows, it's my most precious commodity since becoming a mum.

If this is your first time hearing the words 'cyclical living' and you have no idea of the power your period holds . . . I am beyond *honoured* to share with you what has been lost to us (or withheld from us if you're really into bashing the patriarchy) over the last few generations.

Chapter 3

GOING WITH THE FLOW (LITERALLY)

'When we are in touch with our intuition, our natural cycle and our powers, we are a force to be reckoned with.'

Have you ever discovered something very late on that is so fundamental to the way you live your life and think, *why has nobody told me this before*? This is exactly how I felt when I discovered the art of cyclical living. If the concept of cyclical living is new to you, prepare to have your mind and uterus blown.

I was introduced to cyclical living, which, put simply, is living in tune with your menstrual cycle (and the moon) at the grand old age of 37. Can you *believe* the audacity that 37 is when I truly learnt about periods? Like us all, I spent my youth having regular sex education lessons where we spent more time rolling a condom onto a cucumber than learning about the incredible cycles we will go through for the rest of our lives as women. There was not one mention of the four personalities we were going to have per month, let alone how to work with those energies rather than against them, as so many women have done all their lives. If this sounds familiar, you're not alone – far from it! As a thirty-seven-year-old having had three children, more than three pregnancies and approaching perimenopause . . . *now* I find out how my body really works? It's truly a crime.

Cyclical living is for every woman, whether she still has a

cycle or not, but particularly for those of you who relate to the following:

- If you spend a week each month finding yourself hating your life, thinking you have no friends and wanting to crawl into a hole only to find your period comes the next day and those feelings all go away.
- If you make plans when you're full of energy and wanting to socialise, then, when the day comes around, you find yourself *dreading* the aforementioned plans and find any excuse not to go.
- If you hate the fact you can't be consistent with your workouts as your energy levels vary from day to day. *Why am I so tired?!*
- If you beat yourself up for having a fluctuating appetite and wonder why you can't just be consistent.
- If you fancy your local door-to-door scrap metal dealer who has face tattoos (but only at certain times of the month).
- If you sometimes want to break free from the shackles of motherhood and let loose on the town, but other times want to lie in bed cuddling your kids while also crying to videos of them on your phone.

Let's start to understand how your body *really* works so you can actually have the energy to achieve your goals and start to live your best life!

It's a Man's World, We're Just Living in It

The concept of cyclical living is not new, made up or trendy. It's an ancient practice that our ancestors, the women who

came before us, were well aware of. When there was less artificial light and more community (aka when it was less light and
more lit), women would all cycle together (and I don't mean
the Tour de France!). When it was menstruation time, the women
would retreat together in what was commonly known as 'the
red tent' to rest, nurture themselves and share wisdom, advice
and stories. Throughout time and different cultures, a variation
of this was happening for the good of the women, their families
and communities as a whole. When they reached that point in
their cycle, all they did was rest, nurture and connect – it's so
simple, yet, for so many years, so effective. What a goddamn
dream! Women thrived with this knowledge of their own bodies
and this routine, so why did we lose it? I'll give you one word:
patriarchy. You only need to look at the ways in which women
have been suppressed in the last few hundred years to understand why: when we are in touch with our intuition, our natural
cycle and our powers, we are a force to be reckoned with.

Cyclical living is the practice of getting to know your own
body and honouring what stage of the cycle you are in by
aligning your workload, social life, lifestyle choices, sex life and
self-care rituals with the natural rhythm of your body. Once you
learn to understand and embrace your cycle rather than fight
against it, you get this incredible monthly road map for how
you're going to be feeling and when. This allows you to manage
your energy, productivity, happiness and overall well-being.
Why does this matter when we're talking about manifesting
our dream lives? Because do you know how difficult it can be
to reach your dreams and achieve your goals when you're
exhausted, your emotions are wildly fluctuating and your life
feels overwhelming? It's impossible! Being 'too busy' or 'too
tired' are the top reasons women give me for 'falling off the
manifesting bandwagon'. They *know* it works, but they're just

exhausted from life. That's why getting this right and hacking your hormones is crucial. A lot of the techniques and methods I use to manifest are also just time and energy hacks to allow me the space to create my dream life.

The world in which we live today has been purely designed for the day-to-day circadian rhythm of men – what a surprise! Men's biological systems are governed by the circadian rhythm which is a 24-hour cycle. This cycle regulates everything you can imagine, from sleep, metabolism and energy to mood and hormone production. The circadian rhythm is greatly affected by light, and so exposure to bright sunlight in the morning will kick-start cortisol production, which will make you alert, awake and ready for the day ahead. In the evening, the darkness will signal the body's production of melatonin – the sleepy hormone.

We, too, as women have a circadian rhythm, but our dominant, primary infradian rhythm is our (roughly) 28-day cycle that aligns with the moon. Nevertheless, the modern world and society is set up for men and this rhythm alone, not taking into account the female 28-day cycle at all. Our schools, colleges and workplaces all work on an approximate nine-to-five, Monday to Friday schedule, which is simply not designed for women to thrive.

In order to understand this, we need to look at the key hormone at play here, which is testosterone which both men and women produce, but in very different ways.

For men, testosterone peaks in the morning giving energy and alertness as they start their working day and dips in the evening, which makes it align perfectly with the typical nine-to-five working day. So, off they go, full of energy and raring to go every single morning; however, by 5pm, their daily shot of energy is spent and it's time to retire home for the day and rest, ensuring the same result day after day, month after month, year after year, with very little fluctuation.

For women, the amount of testosterone we produce depends on the time of the month and what stage of our cycle we are in. There will be a couple of days in the month when we are unstoppable and have endless energy, but come the luteal phase (I'll tell you about this in a minute!), there is very little produced which brings on crippling fatigue as well as a whole load of other productivity-inhibiting symptoms. A woman on top of her game one week may feel at the bottom of the heap the next. She isn't inconsistent, she isn't a failure; she's simply a woman trying to fit into a man's world.

As you can see, men can pretty easily fit into this conventional, productivity-focused societal structure. Women, however, will always struggle, as their monthly menstrual cycle is a womb-shaped peg trying to fit into a square hole.

Throughout this monthly cycle, hormones like oestrogen, progesterone and testosterone ebb and flow, influencing energy, productivity, mood, focus and even physical strength. Ignoring these natural fluctuations and forcing a 24-hour schedule on a 28-day cycle can lead to burnout, frustration and a sense of constantly swimming against the tide. Doesn't this all sound very familiar?

OK, so let's go a little deeper into each phase of the cycle and how we can work with it to live a happier and more fulfilling life, because Lord knows, as mums, we need all the help we can get.

Turn Your Body into Your Greatest Ally

If you're ready to change your life and manage your energy like a boss bitch, keep reading. First, you need to get to know the four phases . . .

Menstruation

This is the first phase of the cycle and the one that you can most easily identify by the passing of blood – your period! Your period starts when an egg from the previous cycle isn't fertilised, the levels of oestrogen and progesterone drop, and the lining of your uterus sheds.

During this phase, your energy will retreat inwards and you may find yourself doing a lot of reflection on your life and everything in it. I truly believe that this is both a blessing and a curse. This part of the cycle can be a fucker as you pick arguments with people in your life and find yourself hating your job/home/friends/life (delete as appropriate). It's helpful to recognise this as a hormonal problem, not a life problem. It's likely that if you asked yourself how you felt about the same issue in two weeks' time, you would feel completely different. However, having said this, it is a vital part of our cycle – as our energy turns inwards, we naturally reflect on our lives and what is not in alignment for us will be highlighted (often painfully) to us each and every single cycle.

For example, for me, as I've mentioned, back in 2020, I decided to move from my beloved London where I had chosen to spend the majority of my adult life to the countryside to have a slower way of life and be near family while my daughters were very young. This was absolutely the right thing to do for that season of my life. Being a single parent – hell, any parent – to young children is savage at times and I know that my decision to move somewhere with a big garden, space to play, no traffic, a close community and family support nearby was 100 per cent right for us as a family.

Four years into this new life, though, at every beginning of the menstrual phase, I would start to feel I wasn't in the right place, that my life wasn't in alignment and that I wanted to move back to London. For months and months I would ignore this call and push it down, blaming it purely on hormones. It was only when I went to one of my regular women's circles that an older woman there told us about how these thoughts that repeatedly come up around this time may be difficult to hear, but are begging for our attention. We are being called to reflect on our lives and give attention to what isn't quite working.

Ever since I recognised that and thanked my body, my inner wisdom, the moon, my inner goddess – whatever you want to call it – for highlighting this to me, it settled down. It's no longer something I run and hide from, but speak about openly with friends and family and have plans for in the future. What is your body telling you during this phase? Listen to her. Don't be afraid to face it.

The menstrual phase is for prioritising rest. In fact, this entire phase could have been explained with only two words: rest and reflect. Say no more often, and fiercely protect your time and energy. Going into the menstrual phase then ceases to be a stressful, dreaded time where you feel burnt out, exhausted and sad – but rather a time to embrace, allow yourself to sink down and in, let go of what is not essential and show your family as well as yourself that your physical and mental well-being is a priority. What a gift to not only yourself, but others too.

Follicular phase

This phase starts on the first day of your period (so there is some overlap with the menstrual phase) and lasts roughly 10–14 days right up to ovulation. During this time, the lining of your uterus is thickening, preparing for an egg, which is caused by rising oestrogen levels. This also promotes good mood, energy levels and cognition. This phase is equivalent to 'spring' in nature. This is when your energy is beginning to return, your enthusiasm for life is on the rise, social confidence returns and mental clarity is on point. So, how can you embrace this phase and optimise your lifestyle to work the follicular phase?

Embrace movement. After the rest and rejuvenation of your menstrual phase (aka being absolutely sedentary for the duration of your period while you eat carbs and watch Netflix), it's time to get moving again. This is the best time for high-energy workouts like HIIT, cardio and strength-training. Your hormone levels mean that your energy and recovery levels are at their peak.

The follicular phase is also the ideal time to plan your girls' nights out, meet up with friends and even network. Hello social butterfly! Use your boost in social confidence thanks to good old oestrogen to strengthen both personal and professional relationships. This could be anything from a small business network event to chatting to that interesting new mum in your baby group.

Mentally, you're on fire right now. Your brain's problem-solving and creative capacity is heightened, so harness this energy by planning, brainstorming or learning new skills.

Ovulation

OK, so now we come to my favourite phase of the cycle. Get excited it's . . . *ovulation!* Once you begin to recognise it, you will totally want to optimise this time in any way you can to bring joy, sexiness, adventure, energy and love into your life. Now, if, like me, your baby-making days are well and truly over – like, the shop is shut, the windows are boarded up and there's a for sale sign on the door – then you may think that knowing when you're ovulating isn't relevant to your life. You couldn't be more wrong my friend. I track my ovulation more now than I ever did in my baby-making years for work, social and health reasons, and it's been paying dividends in my life.

Ovulation is the third phase of the menstrual cycle, typically occurring around day 14 of your cycle or the midway point if your cycle is shorter or longer. It's the shortest yet sweetest phase lasting a cruelly short 16–32 hours. Yes, you read that right. The shittiest phase of our cycle (the luteal phase – we'll come to that) when you're feeling all emo and Debbie Downer, crying at adverts on TV, secretly hating your husband and questioning *all* of your life choices, lasts longer than a *Love Island* relationship, an eternal 10–16 days, yet the *party time* phase is not even 2 days. Thanks for that Universe.

This short phase is party central for both you and your uterus. Physically, it's when a mature egg is primed and ready for 'fertilisation' (although I find calling it this puts off Tinder dates) and takes the party bus down your fallopian tube. Mother Nature has made you energetic, confident and magnetic. You know, so we're tricked into procreating and continuing our species. If you're in the market for a new baby, now is your time.

This is the equivalent of 'summer' in nature. This is when you are going to be feeling your most sociable, outward and energetic. You will be magnetic and nothing will stop you! Remember how in your follicular phase the rising oestrogen levels were making you more confident? Well, now they're at their peak, making you immune to social anxiety, shyness, low mood or wallflower syndrome. In addition, you'll experience a rise in testosterone which boosts libido and strength. Incredibly, to top it off, this mix of heightened hormones literally makes us more attractive. Get in!

Workout wise, your endurance and strength is at an all-time high, so high-intensity workouts or weightlifting are the optimal workouts for right now. Plan your biggest events during this time if you can too. If you are a career or business girlie, plan your big meetings or client schmoozing dates in now. If your business or brand involves social media and being the face, this is the time to film and record all your content and represent.

What are you manifesting right now? This natural higher vibration and energy makes it the perfect time to dream big, visualise and manifest! (If this isn't sounding familiar to you, in a cruel twist of fate, approximately 40 per cent of women experience mild to debilitating pain during ovulation. Can we not catch a break?)

If you have a partner and things in the bedroom have slowed down since motherhood, this is the time to rekindle that fire. If you're dating (hello fellow single mums, I see you!), this is a great time to finally get that date out of your DMs and into the real world. As this is nature trying to get you to have a baby, you will be . . . I don't know how else to put this . . . *up for it*! Utilise this time if you find you otherwise have no time, energy or desire for a romantic relationship. This is also your most fertile time, so if you're not in the market for another baby – be careful!

I used to be married and, after several years of co-sleeping with a child, it took a little thoughtfulness and effort to rekindle that flame. If I had known back then what I know now about how I will feel and how my body reacts during different phases of the cycle, it would have been so much easier. No more planning a romantic weekend away without the kids when you're feeling bloated and depressed in the depths of PMS. You know? Strategically speaking, you can plan to spend some time with your partner and your neglected relationship at a time that is going to really work for you. How magical is that? I may be perpetually single (five years and counting at the time of writing), but I'm hoping that, through this chapter, I can save a few relationships!

I honestly cannot stress enough the importance of optimising this phase. As a single mum of three children, I don't go out loads anymore and, when I do, I want to feel energised, social, confident and have fun. There have been times in the past when I have ill-planned a big Christmas night out with my mum friends in the depths of my PMS and all I have wanted to do is take off my heels, lie on the floor and cry. As mums, our social lives often aren't as full as they used to be, so making those nights out and weekends away count is really important to me. That child-free time is precious! Through tracking my ovulation and planning around my cycle, I have managed to have super fun times with friends, find the desire to date again, effortlessly create work I'm really proud of and so much more.

Luteal phase

I've been dreading writing this part because I hate to be the bearer of bad news. However, the key to the luteal phase is understanding and thriving despite its challenges.

As I've mentioned, the luteal phase, as our luck would have it, is the longest phase of the cycle, lasting from ovulation right through to the first day of your period. This is roughly 10–16 days, depending on the length of your cycle. Physically speaking, your body is now eagerly preparing for a potential pregnancy with a significant rise in progesterone. I like to picture my womb all primed and ready for a baby like Mrs Hinch with a new nursery. The carpet has been laid and vacuumed in zigzags, the vintage bunny wallpaper has been hung, the curtains beautifully tied back with big bows, the cot is one of those clear acrylic ones made famous by Khloé Kardashian . . . and then, if there's no baby, your body tears it all up.

The second half of the luteal phase, I feel, is very similar to the menstrual phase. For this reason, I would suggest that, in the first half of the luteal phase, you tie up any loose ends that need seeing to at work and home, say no to overcommitting and conserve your energy so that you can relax a little as the next phase may (not to scare you but . . .) take you down both physically and mentally!

Hormones are fluctuating wildly during this phase, particularly towards the end, as we gear up for menstruation, which leads to common PMS symptoms such as:

Extreme fatigue and lower energy levels

Have you ever wondered why some days you can be super productive and other days you can barely make it out of bed? I used to beat myself up for this *all the time*. Why have I had enough of my children's energy before lunchtime? Why am I falling asleep with them at 7pm only to wake up in the morning with all my clothes on and the lights on downstairs? Now I understand that I was never built to have the same energy levels each day and I go with the flow as much as I can.

As I hit my peak fatigue days (and you don't always need to track and calendar this – your body will tell you when they are), I tend to go easy on myself as a parent. Although I usually like to get the girls outdoors and being active, and have a bit of an iron fist when it comes to iPad use, I let me and them off the hook during this time, allowing them to have some screen time as I take a much-needed rest. We also snuggle up for guilt-free daytime movies – what a treat!

How different it feels to not struggle through these days with toothpicks holding up my eyelids, but to embrace them, slow down and just rest. Close the curtains, get out the blankets and let the kids watch their favourite movie in the middle of the day as you recharge. If your children are school-age, make life easy – swap the walk to school for the car or pick up a take-away rather than cooking. I like to think that this is teaching my daughters something really valuable: that it's OK to rest, it's OK to stop and it's OK to listen to your body.

Irritability and sadness

This is one of the best-known side effects of the luteal phase – the *rage*, the *sadness*! Thankfully, I don't cohabit with a man any more, but, when I did, this is when *all* our arguments would happen. I would start fights out of nowhere and I continue to see my friends do it with their partners too. It's so sad because if more couples understood this was a hormone issue, not a relationship issue, well, things could be so much easier.

I notice in myself that my usual calm, patient demeanour with my children tends to slide away during this phase and I can become snappy and angry, which I *hate* about myself. Keeping a record of my cycle, my symptoms and what triggers them has proven to be super helpful in negotiating this monthly challenge. For example, I know that one of my stress/anger triggers is being in a rush and so I really minimise the amount of places we need to be or the rigidity of our plans during this time. If my girls choose to fanny about going in and out the house to fetch various items we definitely don't need five times before we can finally get going, I will be a lot more relaxed about it if we're going for a walk in the woods rather than getting later and later for a theatre or cinema visit that started ten minutes ago.

I find it useful to speak out loud what I'm feeling with the people around me too. I am incredibly open with my daughters about periods and how I'm feeling during each phase. I will often say to them that I'm getting my period any day now and I'm feeling a bit sad or can get a bit angry, so if I snap at them, that I'm sorry. This is so powerful because, first of all, name it to shame it. I'm not just inside my head, wondering why I feel so angry or blue; instead, I am acknowledging to myself and others why I'm feeling the way I am. There is also scientific evidence to support that simply naming your emotion helps you through it. It's as simple as saying, 'I feel sad today.'

Secondly, I am preparing my family for the fact that I am in my angry/sad stage and I may say things I don't mean or act in ways I am not proud of. And it's OK. I'm not perfect, I'm not a robot and neither should they be when they grow up. I feel like this is going to help them so much as they grow up and experience this for themselves. I ensure I don't only speak about the negatives – I will also say when I'm feeling super happy and energetic due to where I am in my cycle. It's all about balance isn't it? Perhaps I speak about it a little too much, as the other day my middle daughter, Riva, said *very* loudly in the school playground, 'Mum, have you still got blood coming out of your bum?' *The horror*!

As my daughters get older, I would love to explore more ways to talk about cyclical living to young girls at the very beginning of their cycling lives as I truly believe we will become the last generation to learn about this incredible power in our thirties and forties.

Food cravings

During this phase, your food cravings, particularly for carbs and sugar, can rage out of goddamn control! The Deliveroo man becomes my temporary boyfriend during these days, visiting my house more often than anyone I know as late-night pizzas and lunchtime treats are ordered with reckless abandon. Chocolate is another demon of mine and no chocolate aisle in my village shop is left unraided at this time of the month.

Just like with the fluctuating energy levels, I would often find myself frustrated with my lack of discipline and varying hunger levels throughout the month. When I realised a pattern and the reasons for it, I simply went with the flow more, knowing that as I hunker down on my sofa with a bar of chocolate this week, it's very likely that my energy and healthier appetite will return the following week. I now tend to think of my 'healthy living' goals, which include eating a balanced diet and getting regular exercise, as a very much three weeks on, one week off kinda vibe, and that's allowed me to fully embrace who I am at every stage of my cycle, not feel guilty and be reassured that my energy and healthy appetite will return.

Hyper-awareness versus loss of focus and motivation

During the first part of your luteal phase, you may have extra focus and attention to detail, which is ideal for tying up the loose ends in your home, life and business. But, as you continue through the longest part of the cycle into menstruation, you may also experience difficulty focusing and reduced motivation. For this reason, I try to ensure that any time-sensitive work or personal projects are tied up so that I'm able to take a slightly slower pace during this phase. It's naturally a time when I find it hard to get motivated and, when I do, I lack focus and make mistakes, so moving around any commitments or work I can makes a huge difference to me and the amount of energy it takes to complete it.

Your energy levels will begin to descend as your hunger levels begin to rise – it's all taking you back to the beginning of the cycle: menstruation.

The moon and your cycle

As I mentioned earlier, the natural cycle of a woman closely follows the cycle of the moon. Women would traditionally bleed on the new moon when the lunar energy is at its lowest and most inward, and ovulate on the full moon when the energy is at its highest. With the introduction of artificial light, international travel and more solitary lifestyles, women are cycling with all different stages of the moon and none are wrong.

What a trip! Try tracking your mood throughout your cycle so that you can begin to recognise patterns. There is a fantastic app available called Stardust which has been instrumental in helping me to understand my own mind, body and cycle. Not only does it track your cycle, but it gives you daily reminders on what's going on, gives an easy-to-understand graph of rising and falling hormones and even tracks the cycle of the moon at the same time! Recognising and identifying repeating feelings or behaviours helps you to prepare for energy and mood dips as well as capitalise on the highs.

By embracing and fully understanding cyclical living, we as women can begin to powerfully harness the strengths of each phase of the cycle rather than feeling confused, frustrated and attempting to override them. With this information, which has been denied to us for generations, we are able to work smarter, not harder, be a better mum, partner and friend, as well as give ourselves permission to *rest*. Whether you are trying to manifest a better relationship, more high-vibe friends, a successful career or more time with your family, harnessing and understanding your energy cycle will transform your life. Over time, you will improve your relationships, boost health, reduce stress and anxiety, and become the woman you always wanted to be.

You've discovered how your hormones and body can support you to manifest your dream life, but what about another ally which may have been acting as more of an enemy? Yes, it can be the biggest source or stress or the biggest source of joy – it's up to you. It is, of course, your home. As mothers, our homes mean far more to us now than when we were bachelorettes. So let's find out . . . what is your home doing to help you?

Chapter 4

AN ENVIRONMENT FOR SUCCESS

'Small environmental changes make a huge impact on how you live out your daily life.'

Something I have discovered over the years and that became more apparent as I transitioned into motherhood is that my environment has a huge impact on me, my quality of life, how I interact with others and my ability to reach my goals. In short, how you design and organise your home can support what kind of life you want to live.

For so many, their home can be a source of stress, anxiety and misery. A cramped, poorly designed or downright depressing home badly organised and filled to the brim with clutter is not an environment from which you can manifest your dream life. After all, your dream life is happening, day by day, here in the present – not on one particular day in the distant future.

I recently went to a book launch for the wonderful David Larbi who wrote a fantastic book called *Frequently Happy*. He spoke that day about finding it easy to be happy on holiday or the day you get engaged, but those days are few and far between. How much better it would be to be able to experience joy and happiness in the everyday. Creating a beautiful, nourishing home helps you feel that everyday joy.

Using your home to support you in living the life you desire is such a satisfying endeavour. Your home will begin to nourish and support your highest version of yourself in two ways:

1. Your home affects how you *behave* (physical).
2. Your home affects how you *feel* (mental).

Physical cues

As you design and curate your environment with physical cues, set-ups and even limitations, it will guide your behaviours. You still need to have conscious thought and decisions to make the good behaviour changes happen, but your home will assist and guide you.

An example of this is I have had a treadmill for about two years now and it's something that, miraculously, I use *all the time*. As the mother to toddler twins who refused to be in a pushchair, the chances of me being able to go out and enjoy a brisk walk were slim to none. I tried it all – scooters, bikes . . . and it often ended in tantrums and a refusal to move. So, to get my daily steps in, I invested in a treadmill and set it up in the dead space behind my sofa, pointed towards the TV. It was always plugged in, set up and ready to go. As a result, I used it almost every day – and still do. It has helped me so much with my health goals.

Recently, I got asked to collaborate with a company to promote them and I jumped at the chance as I love mine so much. I moved it out of the space behind the sofa and placed it in an aesthetically-pleasing part of my kitchen where I could film reels and have it perfectly lit. Since moving it there, I have not used it once. The habit I had built and that worked for me was that, as I watched TV, I would walk. When that cue was taken away, I simply didn't use it. This is how powerful our environment is.

What about the most popular goal of all – to eat healthier as a family? I've found that placing fresh fruit on display in easy-to-reach places makes it an effortless and tempting snack. I also have a little ritual of having a family fruit and crudité platter each evening – and it's the only food that is allowed to be eaten on the sofa, while watching TV. I'm not usually one for mindless eating, but I've noticed just how much fresh fruit and vegetables the girls consume if it's there to graze on during their favourite TV show.

Perhaps the simplest environment hack of them all is to keep a full flask of lemon water, a selection of supplements, eye cream and hand cream on my desk, so that during phone calls or between tasks its super easy to use them. I find otherwise they just get forgotten about and not used.

What goal would you like to achieve, and can you think of an environmental cue that could make it so much easier? Do it today – your future self will thank you for it.

Mental cues

The second way your home environment will influence you and help you manifest your goals is by changing the way you *feel*. What we wake up and see first thing in the morning, the environment in which we live out our daily lives, the items we use on a daily basis – these all either inspire or depress us.

To manifest certain things into our lives we must first *feel* and *embody* them. Back when I was living in that very small, outdated house with the gross, stained brown carpets throughout, it was depressing – it had a barely functioning kitchen with no room for a fridge-freezer. It was around this time that I started my law of attraction podcast and book club, and we read several books on money mindset. I decided that both my home and I must embody that I am a Wealthy Woman. I capitalise 'Wealthy Woman' because the words were said with such emphasis. As I proclaimed to my mum and sister with enthusiasm that I was going to become the wealthiest woman our family had ever seen, I would make a W sign with my hands to emphasise the

Ws. Back then, it seemed funny, me saying that with such belief, as I was the youngest and poorest of the family, living off the self-employed grants from Boris with no business to go back to, every hour of my day and every ounce of my energy taken up by my newborn babies.

Saying 'I am a Wealthy Woman' and looking around my home, there was a dissonance. I didn't live like a Wealthy Woman, nor could I afford to turn my tiny home into a dream home . . . yet. What I did do was slowly, slowly, as I could afford it, change things that made me feel poor.

My kitchen was *gross*, but I couldn't afford a new one, so I spent a weekend and about £30 painting it pink and gold. It was still tiny, it was still old, but it felt better. My two and a half bedrooms were minute and wardrobes are expensive, so I turned our third (half) bedroom into an Instagram-worthy dressing room. I got a local handyman to hang some rails and make an IKEA unit look fitted, placed my oversized mirror up against the window and ta-da – we had our very own dressing room! That felt so fucking boujee. It became my favourite room of the house to hang out in, organise and even take my Instagram selfies in! It was also incredibly efficient as putting the entire family's clothes away into one room is a home hack that every mum needs to know. We now live in a much bigger house with everyone's clothes in their own rooms and I often reminisce about that dressing room wishing it were that simple to put laundry away again. If you have young children and a spare box bedroom, I *highly* recommend turning it into a family dressing room.

With every small change I made along the way, I started to embody that Wealthy Woman. It was easy to wake up and feel like a Wealthy Woman as I got dressed in my gorgeous dressing room. Soon, the changes became bigger and bigger. I realised my battered old wooden front door made me feel poor and so

I changed it for a modern, powder pink one which I adorned with a pink hydrangea wreath. Then, every day as I walked in through my front door, I felt like a Wealthy Woman.

I doubled the floor space in the cramped sitting room by throwing out the bulky TV unit I had bought at a boot sale for £5 and instead hanging the TV on the wall, which enabled me to move the sofa to a much better position. It felt like a new room! Eventually, I got the builders in and added a large kitchen extension with bifold doors and my dream kitchen – finally big enough for a fridge-freezer!

Two years later, I now sit in my dream home (which isn't that house!) which I bought, extended and renovated all within the year. I truly believe that making these small, incremental improvements to my previous home played a big part in being able to achieve this – this home, which takes most working couples a lifetime or more to achieve – in two short years. I woke up and felt like a Wealthy Woman every day because my home reflected that back to me and reinforced it.

As I read that back, I realise that there will be some mothers reading this who are not yet in a position to make bigger changes like those I've listed or who are renting and so are unable to make modifications. It reminds me that often the most effective changes at the start of this journey can be as simple as decluttering, cleaning and mood-setting.

When I first got divorced, Bohemia, who was two at the time, and I moved out from our beautiful family home which overlooked a marina with geese in the back garden and a new kitchen ... back into my bachelorette flat in London. It was a cosy one-bedroom, on top of a rowdy Arsenal pub and far away from our family and support network. I was very aware that this little girl had gone from living in a house with her parents with a garden in a cute gated community to this much different space and I was eager to make it feel as homely and comfortable as possible.

I kept the space ruthlessly decluttered and so it never felt like we were living in 500 square feet. We lived simply, yet beautifully (more on decluttering and creating space in Chapter 5). I did a lot of mood-setting when having dinner or doing her bed and bath routine – low lighting, the diffuser on with organic essential oils for sleep and relaxing spa music in the background. I even found some light-up ice cubes for cocktails that I would put in her bath and then turn the overhead lights off. The spa music drowned out the cheers and boos from the pub below us as Arsenal either scored or lost, and it truly felt like an elevated home experience for both of us. Changes you make to your home don't have to be big, pricey or permanent.

It's not about the size – it's what you do with it

A note on the size of your home in case you're reading this thinking, 'Well, it's OK for you, with your dream home!' I've lived, as I said, in a one-bedroom flat, sharing a bed and a wardrobe with Bohemia. I now live in a large home with more than enough bedrooms for everyone (not that they bloody sleep in them!), large, open-plan living spaces, a play room, a home office, a garage, a large garden . . . and I've realised that there are positives and negatives to each side of the coin.

I often reminisce about our simple days living in that flat with little space or storage. We were very intentional with what we brought home. Bohemia had one basket of toys and, without sounding like we were living through the Second World War, we had one colouring book with a paint palette and two paintbrushes. We would sit after dinner and paint together most nights. We would cook together, we would do yoga on the TV and we went outside a lot. My home took almost no time to clean and organise. Life was good!

With a bigger home comes a lot more ease with having space for more toys, more crafts and storage, but it also magnetises clutter and chaos if you're not careful. It now takes half a day and reinforcements to clean and clear my home, so I guess what I'm saying is, it doesn't matter how large, small, fancy or shabby your home is, the energy and effort you put into making it a clean, clear, intentional space will reap dividends and will have far more of an impact on your quality of life than your square footage or postcode.

Creating an Environment to Support You

I would love for you to think about what goals you would like to achieve in your life and how your environment could support that. I'm going to give you some examples of how my home has helped me in the hope that you are inspired to try it yourself.

Mindset

One of my goals for 2024 was to look at my phone less. I am a stickler for the kids not being on screens, and yet I was being pulled into my phone more than ever. There were moments when I found myself craving a mindless scroll – while the girls were playing Barbies and just wanted me nearby, through endless soft play sessions or during the nightly 'witching hour' when *Peppa Pig* or *Peter Rabbit* would be on repeat. Instead of sneaking out my phone and feeling terrible that I was now *that* mother, more consumed by her phone than her child, I used the strategic placement of books and read. It quelled my boredom, enabled me to be there physically for the girls, nourished my soul *and* was an incredible example to set to my girls. Did I want them to see me staring at a phone for hours a day, or habitually being engrossed in a book during certain downtimes? Absolutely.

If your goal is also to read more, set up your environment so that choosing books is easy and obvious. I have books in our car, with more grown-up, interactive ones in the passenger seat for Bohemia to ask me questions as we drive. On my coffee table in my sitting room, I have a pile of seasonal, curated coffee table books to peruse at any given time. You're likely to be interrupted so there are no long, complicated novels, but fascinating hardbacks on London architecture, the life of Amy Winehouse, *hygge* (the Danish art of cosy, feel-good connection), Banksy, how to live like an aspirational French woman – you name it! The placement of these books has given me so much time back to just read for pleasure again.

Imagine what goals you could achieve through reading more. Whether it's for education, to learn a new skill, to set up a new business or just to provide some much-needed nervous system resetting, reading is a fabulous addition to any day. Where in your home would you most benefit from keeping a book or two? Do you get nap-trapped on your sofa every afternoon or find yourself sitting in your car waiting for football training or dance classes to finish? Maybe you're sitting outside bedroom doors each night until the kids are asleep. All these situations are magnets for mindless scrolling, which isn't improving your life. Imagine the compound effect of taking that time back and doing something positive with it! This helps with manifesting in so many ways. Not only is less time being sucked into our screens going to free our minds up to create the life of our dreams, but it also feeds into a healthy, positive self-identity, which is *vital* for upgrading your life. You can confidently feel like, 'I'm the kind of bitch who reads every day' and doesn't that feel *great*?

Taking another example, if you want to start each day with the powerful practice of writing a gratitude list or journaling (which I highly recommend, by the way), the best way I've found is to keep a notebook and pen beside your bed, in full view. It makes it easy, visible and actually quite attractive as choosing to spend ten minutes writing means an extra ten minutes cocooned in your cosy bed.

Health

One of my New Year mottos was 'health is wealth'. Something I'd noticed about myself was that I *always* forgot to take my vitamins and supplements. So, I bought a pill box with daily compartments and filled up the box with all the pills I would need each week on a Sunday night. I kept the box in a prominent place on my desk and ta-da – I was able to take the supplements that my severely depleted body needed (twin breastfeeding took a goddamn toll – I not only lost a huge amount of weight, but also a tooth for good measure).

Growing up with disordered eating (I've still never eaten a sandwich and I'm 40), I find the routine of meal planning, shopping for food and cooking tough to say the least. It doesn't come naturally to me and I can often end up in a weird 'girl dinner' routine of eating a bowl of peas and a packet of crisps. I have made several set routines to beat this including meal planning as I plan my week on a Sunday night, food shopping as a ritual with my daughters every Monday and keeping my kitchen clean, clear and set up for me to achieve my home-cooking goals. I also have a recipe book full of meals that I don't need to know how to make as I've done them so many times; I just need to be reminded sometimes of the meals I *can* cook.

Often goals like 'lose weight' or 'eat healthier' are so hard to stick to – they seem like such a mammoth task, but really it all comes down to making some simple micro changes to our everyday lives to see massive compound results further down the line. For me, my biggest goal of 'health is wealth' boiled down to some very simple actions:

1. Plan my week out, including a meal plan on a Sunday night.
2. Food shop every Monday with a proper list of everything I need.
3. Get the children involved so that I have accountability.

That's it! By putting these simple steps in place, I had built a habit which is now an effortless part of my weekly routine.

What is the biggest hurdle for you reaching your health goals? Is your diet or movement in need of some attention? How could your environment support you? We often put 'being healthy' as this huge, unattainable, vague-as-fuck goal but don't think about the simple steps required to get us there. Start small – so small it's impossible to fail – and repeat.

Self-care

When my twins were newborns, and probably up until they were two, life was very, very difficult. I found that even my simple self-care rituals of washing my face at night and brushing my teeth were impossible to keep up with. I soon realised that it was my environment that was making it difficult, and therefore it was also my environment that could make it easy.

In the mornings after a broken night's sleep of breastfeeding and co-sleeping, it was always a rush for school. I would get all the girls downstairs and then, if I tried to go up to wash my face or use any of my products, everyone would cry and try to follow me up the stairs. The way my stairs were designed, it was impossible to have a stair gate at the bottom, only the top. This meant that, during the day, while the girls were awake, I simply couldn't get or use any of my personal care products unless I wanted to carry two heavy, crawling babies up the stairs with me each time. Forget it, it was too much hard work!

In the evenings, I would put all my daughters to bed and then creep back downstairs for a couple of hours to myself to work on my podcast or maybe watch the latest episode of Love Island (don't judge me – we all need a little escape and that was as close to a holiday as I was going to get for a while). Once it was time to go up to bed, I would be faced with the dilemma of brushing my teeth and washing my face, risking waking them all up with the noise, or just going straight to bed with the hope of a few precious moments more sleep. Let me save you any guesswork: the extra sleep won every time! Soon enough, I was suffering with my skin as it was desperately uncared for. Then, I had the idea to create what I call a 'mum cupboard' in my kitchen, our most used room. The mum cupboard had everything I needed to take care of myself and feel looked after. I had my toothbrush and paste, skincare, body moisturiser, pills, nail clippers – even my make-up bag – all there in one place!

That simple shift made the biggest difference. All of a sudden, I was able to give my skin the care and attention it

MANIFEST LIKE A MOTHER

needed while the girls played at my feet or while cooking the dinner and I could brush my teeth while the girls had their breakfast. It was all just so much easier.

When you begin to prioritise yourself, even in the smallest of ways, you send a powerful message to your subconscious that you are worthy of care, love and abundance. It's not just about bubble baths and candles (although if that brings you joy, go for it). It's about recognising your own needs as valid and essential, rather than something to be squeezed in after everyone else has been taken care of. When you nourish yourself, physically, emotionally and mentally, you shift into a place of alignment where manifesting becomes second nature.

So as you move forward, take a moment to ask yourself: how can I show up for myself today in a way that proves I am worthy of my dreams? The answer doesn't have to be grand. It might be taking five minutes alone with a cup of tea, going to bed an hour earlier or simply reminding yourself that you deserve ease, joy and success. These small acts build momentum and, before you know it, you're no longer just dreaming of a better life – you're living it.

Work

Before I moved house and created my home office, I had to work anywhere and everywhere I could sit with my laptop and microphone. Before the girls were old enough to start going to nursery, I had to rely on the couple of hours in the evenings once they were in bed to get everything done. The laptop had a permanent home on the arm of my sofa, so that I could also grab it and record during the day while I was feeding or the girls were having a nap.

The problem came during the evening when I wanted to make the most of that time and work. I would come downstairs and, instead of grabbing my laptop, I would sit on the sofa and turn on the TV – it's the way the room was designed. The remote was right there and the sofa was pointing towards the focal point of the room – the TV. I realised I had to break that habit if I was going to get anything done, and so I started setting up my laptop, microphone and notebook on my dining table before I took the girls upstairs. I plugged in the laptop, turned it on and left it open. I made it as easy as possible to go and sit there to work. I would even leave myself a little snack on the table to enjoy when I came down. It suddenly meant that, when I stumbled down those stairs a few hours later (why does bedtime take so long?), bone weary from another day of hardcore mothering, I gave myself a fighting chance of making the right decision. The right decision, of course, being to go and work on my laptop rather than sit and watch TV. (I just want to point out that when I say make 'the right decision', I don't want this to come off as hustle culture. There are absolutely nights when 'the right decision' is to flop on the sofa and *rest*. However, in that stage of my life, I was determined to completely transform my miserable little life into one I was proud of – and that took concentrated effort.)

If my procrastination resonates with you, I have found something that really helps: remove every bit of friction holding you back from making an excuse. In this example, it could have been that I didn't know where the charger was, it was a stretch to plug it in behind a piece of furniture or I couldn't find the book I was working from . . .

Look around at your own life – where is friction slowing you down? Where are those tiny, seemingly insignificant obstacles adding up to keep you stuck? Maybe it's the pile of unfolded laundry on the chair that makes your workspace feel chaotic, draining your energy before you've even started your day.

Maybe it's digging through an overstuffed drawer every morning to find your charger, making the simple act of getting going feel like a chore. Or maybe it's scrolling on your phone late at night, making it harder to wake up early and do the things you promised yourself you would.

These tiny obstacles might seem insignificant on their own, but they add up, creating just enough resistance to stop you from following through. When something feels like a hassle, even in the smallest way, your brain will take the path of least resistance, often leading you away from the habits and actions that move you closer to your goals.

What would happen if you made things easier for yourself; if you set up your environment to support you instead of subtly working against you? Imagine waking up to a tidy workspace, your laptop out ready to go, your journal waiting with a fresh page. Imagine opening your fridge to find healthy meals prepped, your vision board in clear sight, your home arranged in a way that inspires you rather than overwhelms you. These aren't just little tweaks – they are signals to yourself that you are worthy of ease, of progress, of success. You don't need to force yourself to be more disciplined or work harder. You just need to clear the path so that the version of you who already has everything you desire can step forward effortlessly.

What small adjustments could make your daily routines feel smoother and more aligned with the future you're creating? Often, the difference between staying stuck and moving forward is as simple as making the right choice the easiest one to make.

Connection

One aspect of my home life I really wanted to focus on was for my home to be the backdrop of a connected family life as well as a full social life.

We've all been to people's parties and homes where it simply doesn't flow – people are disconnected and it doesn't lend itself to the art of gathering. My home used to be this! Before I renovated, knocked down walls and extended, my house was a warren of small rooms, none fit for purpose. Friends and family would come in, walk down a narrow corridor into my kitchen where I would make them a drink and then it wouldn't be obvious where to sit: either the dining room that depressed me and wasn't near any of the kids' toys so they wouldn't stay there or the sitting room where there wasn't enough room for everyone to sit. What a choice! I knew what I needed to do and it involved a sledgehammer. I opened up the whole space, joined the kitchen and dining room together and moved the entrance of the kitchen closer to the sitting room so that it all felt like one big space that flowed. I designed everything around feeling and connection.

I also did a lot of research on dining tables after making a pricey mistake. I saw this beautiful driftwood and glass dining table online which I *had to have*. It had a three-month delivery date, but, when it arrived, I was devastated! Yes, it looked beautiful, but something I hadn't anticipated was that the glass top was hard, cold to the touch, not to mention less than ideal with messy kids' fingerprints. Not my most intelligent purchase, so off to Facebook Marketplace I went.

I realised then that a dining table is more than just a table – it's such an important centrepiece for family life. In a world where people are busier and busier, preferring to eat alone or in their rooms, it was more crucial than ever for me to cultivate a desirable mealtime environment where my family and friends would want to gather.

First things first, it must be easy and obvious to use, so having it tucked away in a formal dining room wasn't going to be right for me – placing it in the kitchen simply worked better. After my mistake with the glass table, I realised that how the table felt was an important factor and only a cosy wood would do. No glass, no metal, no marble – just warm to the touch, characterful wood. I then discovered the psychology of round tables.

Round tables are often considered better for encouraging connection and conversation because of several psychological and practical factors. We've all been to that big group dinner where you've been stuck at one end, unable to hear the conversation further down the table. Worse still, you're on the end with nobody else opposite you. When that happens to me, I pretty much want to turn around and go home. With a round table, there is completely equal seating with everyone equidistant and no head of the table. Nobody is left stuck in the corner or left out of conversation, which often happens with rectangular tables. Eye contact and conversation is effortless as everyone is able to see without needing to lean forward, turn their heads or block another person. Not only this, but circles of people are associated with intimacy and unity – just think about women's circles. It's even been noted time and again that people seated at round tables in restaurants stay longer and have a better experience. The inclusive design of a round table encourages conversation, laughter and deeper connections. When people feel more engaged socially, they are less likely to rush through the meal or feel the urge to leave. As mothers who clearly want a family life filled with daily connection, this is such a simple way to achieve it.

And so, as you can imagine, with a round dining table and soft, comfy dining chairs, I suddenly had a kitchen dining space that was begging to be enjoyed – whether that was for several hours over a Sunday roast, a Chinese takeaway or even an afternoon cup of tea. I saw this in action the first time my mum came round after its purchase. Usually, my elderly mother would find it difficult to sit on a hard chair, but, ironically, found my sofa too soft, and so, after some perching, she wouldn't stay long. The day I got my dining area set up, we sat and chatted around that table for hours. The round table is magic!

Think about your own dining set-up. It's such an easy and effective area of your home to work on because the rewards will continue to flow. I love anything that has a compound effect. Think about it – you change your cold, glass table for a cosy round one, you invest in some comfortable seats, you have a radio or smart speaker nearby so you can have relaxing music on for mealtimes and the flickering glow of a candle on the table. Every single day, your family mealtime has been trans-formed into a family ritual – a time not to be rushed or endured but enjoyed, together.

We often set lofty, vague goals of 'spending more quality time as a family' or 'feeling connected to my partner each day', but don't know how to realistically get there. The secret isn't a family trip spent trying to prise devices away from the kids or a romantic getaway with your partner that took military-style planning to get organised with childcare, and so on – it's achieved through the small, daily habits – like eating together – that your home can support you with.

Fun

Now, I know this is going to sound a little boujee, but one of my favourite things about living in London was being able to hang out at Shoreditch House pool on a hot day. The Soho House private members' club rooftop pool was a goddamn *vibe*, whether I was having an early-morning swim and pool-side breakfast with Bohemia or an all-day rosé wine with ma tits out in the pool situation with friends. It genuinely brought me so much joy and I would fully like my funeral to be held there if at all possible. I sacrificed so much and worked so hard during that period of my life, being a single mum for the first time, sharing a bedroom, working ridiculously long hours and renting out my home to make my country house dream happen, but that members' club was one luxury I kept. It was important for my mindset and for my identity.

When I moved to the countryside, I was so sad to leave it behind, so I made it my mission to replicate that feeling the best I could. My biggest goal for 2023 was to turn my garden into a summer haven for us and our friends and family. I visualised birthday pool parties for my daughters, family BBQs on weekends and all-day, into-the-night parties on my child-free weekends.

I know that this is taking it slightly too far, but at the bottom of my garden, overlooking fields and where the sun lingered the longest, I fully invested in a 19-foot swim spa, dug into the ground and surrounded by decking. I was ready for pool party fun! But the great British outdoors can be harsh and I often found myself not naturally wanting to spend much time in my garden and wondered why. Through lots of pool days with family and pool parties with friends, I soon discovered that the harsh sun, a cold breeze or the loss of light as evening came could cut a perfectly good pool party day short. I set out to learn what I needed to provide to make it a more comfortable place to hang out.

Comfy seating was a must, so I got an outdoor sofa and table set with big, squishy cushions and laid out blankets on the arms. I also invested in double sun loungers, almost the size of a double bed, for the sun worshippers to lie on and relax.

In the UK, you never know if you're going to get a heatwave or a rainstorm, so I put in place a large parasol suitable for both. The shade and rain cover it provides have both been used equally! Something I noticed that cut short garden parties was the loss of light at around 9 or 10pm. Suddenly, we found ourselves in the pitch black at the bottom of my garden with absolutely no lights around in my countryside village. When I purchased my parasol, a friend recommended one that had in-built solar lights and it's been a goddamn game changer. That, along with the fire pit table which provides both light and heat to gather around, has been the hero in keeping the parties going until the early hours.

The fact is, you don't need a dug-in pool to enjoy your garden, but it *did* give me a reason to get people to gather and enjoy the summers. By providing a place to get together, comfortable seating, a focal point, protection from the sun and rain, and light in the evenings, my garden is the backdrop to many happy memories as I look back at the end of each year. It's completely setting up my environment for fun that has created that magic.

How could you create this feeling in your own space? Perhaps you already have the perfect nook or hangout that's rarely used. Identify a cosy, comfortable area ideal for connection and fun. It might need sweeping, cleaning or rejigging, but commit to enjoying the space with friends or family in the next week if you can. Remember, our homes don't need to be Instagram-worthy, pristine or show homes – just a comfortable place where friends and family feel happy hanging out. One of my best ever garden parties was at that weird stage of lockdown where you were allowed to meet friends but it had to be outside and nobody could touch. My mum friends all brought a deck chair each and we pooled our alcohol and snacks for the evening into a cardboard box which we placed in the middle of us. We chatted and laughed well into the night and, when it got too dark, we burnt old broken-up fence panels on a tiny, rusty fire pit from B&M. *This* is true *hygge*, and style has nothing to do with it.

How Does Your Home Make You Feel?

When I was hunting for my dream home to raise my daughters in, I decided that not only did it need to be a homely, cosy sanctuary, as well as practical for our family (for example, close to school, enough bedrooms for all the girls and a garden big enough for a bouncy castle on birthdays), but it also needed to make me feel rich. I know that sounds wild, but money mindset is something that I'm so passionate about (see Chapter 12 for more on this!). I knew that if my home didn't make me feel like a rich, successful bad bitch every time I walked into it, my power to manifest money would be decreased. As a single-income household, money is *very* important to me. I specifically needed the hallway of my new home to feel luxurious. Think Kris Jenner in the early noughties with double-height ceilings, a grand staircase and a chandelier.

As I viewed house after house, I was increasingly disappointed with the state of the hallways. Even in the larger, more expensive homes I viewed, they had pokey, off-centre hallways that didn't match the price tag. I even tried to talk a developer into letting me knock out an upstairs en suite to make the depressing hallway double height in a new build I viewed. He thought I was crazy. I get it – UK homes aren't the largest, so why would you waste precious square footage on a room that doesn't need to be anything other than a place to take off your shoes?

I put on my 'dream home' vision board a beautiful hallway and gallery landing with a strong oak staircase, feature windows and a central chandelier hanging in the chasm. After viewing what felt like 100 houses, I found The One. It was a large house with an oversized, double-height hallway with a gallery landing and oversized chandelier in the middle – *just* like my vision board! What was wild was that beyond that grand hallway was the smallest, old-fashioned kitchen. It was like they had prioritised and built the entire house around this grand hallway. I was sold!

I renovated and extended the house to become my dream living space, and every time I walk into it I feel successful and abundant, so I created the hallway of my dreams to remind me to embody being a successful, Wealthy Woman every time I entered or left my home.

I started with the entrance to the hallway, dressing the front door with a beautiful, seasonal wreath and box topiary either side as you enter. Straight away, as I drive up to my house I often think, 'Wow, this is some real Mrs Hinch shit' and it brings me *joy*! As you step inside, the walls have been painted a calming, neutral hessian colour and the floor is a rich oak herringbone. There's a natural driftwood console table to the side bearing gold photo frames filled with happy memories from our family life. I've heard it's very beneficial for children to see photos of themselves placed around the home – it supports their self-worth and self-esteem. I hope that, in addition to this, the pictures I've chosen from our travels around the world or sunny days in the garden with family evoke happy memories for them on the dullest of days.

There are bursts of life thanks to plants in matching wicker baskets, including a Japanese money plant by the front door for prosperity (yes, I'm a feng shui bitch too!). On the wall hangs a beautiful artwork by Real Hackney Dave featuring an oversized vintage map of Cornwall overlaid with real gold leaf proclaiming 'CORNWALL IS ALWAYS A GOOD IDEA'. I started buying random art I loved when the podcast first took off and I bought that particular piece in a gallery in the swanky fishing village (those words don't seem to go together do they?) of Padstow. Every time I look at that piece, I'm reminded of a happy holiday spent with family, doing nice, boujee shit and feeling so content.

I would love for you to give your environment some thought and attention. How does it make you behave? How does it make you feel?

Show gratitude for your home

Above my doorway hangs a framed, symbolic £50 note with the words 'Thank you for all the money I have been given in my life' on it. This was one of the first gratitude practices I learnt with the law of attraction and I framed that note when I had very little. It graced my cramped, old hallway before I visualised it hanging in the hallway of my dream home – which it now does.'

Every time I walk into my home, I genuinely feel gratitude for this beautiful house which protects me, my daughters and our belongings, and gives us a place from which to achieve so many of our goals. I recently spoke to a fellow author on my podcast and she remarked that from social media she had seen how loved my home was and what it provided for us. She called it a 'fortress of love' and I took that name and ran with it. It *is* a fortress of love. It's been designed to be our sanctuary, our refuge – as everybody needs from the outside world; a place to restore, reset, rest and nourish. But, more than that, it's a home to share, to invite loved ones into and do life together. I'm so thankful to my home for providing that for us.

I have so much gratitude for my home that I often speak to it, thanking it as I leave the driveway for looking after all of our possessions, for its protection on a cold, stormy night, for the safe space it provides for my children to play in the sun, for giving my friends a place to stay – for so many things. This came from a book I read by Marie Kondo called *The Life-Changing Magic of Tidying* where I discovered the concept of Shinto. Shinto is the indigenous spiritual tradition of Japan, centred around the worship of *kami* – sacred spirits or deities believed to inhabit nature, objects and even human-made structures, aka your home. In essence, the belief is that some objects, especially those that have been used and cherished for a long time, are thought to develop a spiritual essence of their own.

Bear with me, I know this sounds wild, but have you ever walked into a house and thought it has either a good or bad vibe? Have you ever wondered why the homes of serial killers are demolished with even the bricks being ground to dust? I truly believe that homes have a soul and we can work with them in gratitude to increase our fortune.

I remember I was getting pretty deep into this shit around the time when I was moving from my old home. That little house had been the guinea pig for a lot of my manifesting rituals and experiments – was it any coincidence that it was also the backdrop to the biggest metamorphosis in my life? I began to get very emotional about leaving that home which had nurtured me through some of the darkest times of my life and decided to start a new gratitude ritual for whenever I left a home.

On my moving day, I sat and wrote a letter to my house. It was filled with gratitude for everything it had provided for me and my babies – the shelter it had given us, the warmth, the strength, the space to live a life that was beyond my dreams. I cried as I wrote it, folded it up, kissed it and threw it into my loft hatch, never to be found hopefully! Just as I did, my lights began to flicker on and off. I shit you not, it happened. In that moment I *knew* it was the energy of the house acknowledging my gratitude. I honestly had never had a power cut or any-thing in that house before, so for the lights to flicker at that very moment? I'm sold.

And so, how can you incorporate some more gratitude for your home into your life? Remember, even if your home isn't your ideal home right now, what we have gratitude for must grow. Showing gratitude for every home you have, regardless of how small, unsuitable or old-fashioned it is, is the key to living your most abundant and happy home life.

Create a home that holds you

As a mother, our homes are even more important to us than to most. When I look back on how I treated my little London flat in my twenties, I was barely there – it was somewhere to rest my head at night and an address to order pizza to. Now, my home has become my greatest ally in the daily endeavour to nurture my children and myself. It helps me parent as it provides a place to play, to socialise, to cook, to eat and to rest.

As we spend our days caregiving, working from home post-pandemic and enjoying nights in with friends rather than nights out due to childcare, our homes are now not *just* our homes, but our workplaces, social clubs and offices too. How can your home help you become the best mother you can be, but also achieve your personal goals?

Imagine a day in the life of a poorly designed home environment.

You wake up groggy from a bad night's sleep because your bedroom is overstimulating and a catch-all for laundry, ironing piles and redundant exercise equipment. You have to squeeze past bottles and bottles of precariously balanced products to get into the shower. You battle with a wardrobe overstuffed with out-of-season clothes to find something to wear for the day, resorting to the same leggings and sweatshirt combo for the 2,000th day running. Breakfast is stressful because you haven't cleaned up the kitchen from the night before.

It's a work-from-home day, so you flop onto the sofa, turn on the TV for background noise and attempt to work while getting distracted. The children come home from school and watch TV or game because it's the first thing they see. At dinner time, you end up eating the same pasta dish or getting a take-away because you don't have the space in your kitchen or the energy to try new recipes. The dining table is cluttered and so you and whoever you live with eat separately, facing the TV or your phone screen, your relationships stagnating or deteriorating with each passing day. You skip your much-needed self-care night because you can't remember where you put the bath salts and face masks.

OK, so that's a pretty extreme example, but I bet there are elements of that day that are familiar for you.

Now, imagine your home being fully optimised for you to live out your ideal day. Your home assists and supports you in achieving your goals and fulfilling your intentions.

You wake up rested and restored from an incredible night's sleep. You move to the bathroom where you easily find and use all the products you need to begin your day feeling fresh and clean. You dress for the life you want, picking from a curated closet of in-season clothes that fit and flatter you. Breakfast is healthy and easily accessible from a clean, organised kitchen.

You begin your working day in a designated 'work space' that is inspiring, free from distractions and set up to encourage productivity. The children come home from school or nursery to a small selection of rotated toys or to craft supplies set out, and immediately get stuck into them, happily playing together.

Dinner is a new recipe you're trying as you have the capacity to try new foods in a clean and clear, functional kitchen. The family enjoys mealtime rituals together around a cosy dining table which has been lit with candles as they ask each other about their days. In the evening, you relax into a deep bath and listen to an audiobook or podcast which nourishes and restores you mind, body and soul. You get into bed and prepare for a deep, restful sleep which will give you all the energy you need for tomorrow.

Again, this is an extreme version and, of course, there are days when your kids see the crafts and flip the table regardless or you're exhausted and get a Deliveroo despite your best intentions. However, the vast majority of the time, these small environmental changes make a huge impact on how you live out your daily life.

The key is to make it as easy as possible to do the things you say you want to do. If you want to read more, place your book where you'll see it instead of buried under a pile of laundry. If you want to work out in the morning, lay out your clothes the night before. If eating healthier is your goal, prep your meals or snacks in advance so you're not reaching for whatever is quickest when hunger strikes. These small shifts remove decision fatigue and make progress feel effortless.

To bring it all together, let's think about what this truly means for you. Your home is not just a backdrop to your life – it's an active participant in your success. It holds the energy of your daily routines, your aspirations and your moments of rest. When you intentionally shape your environment to support your goals, you remove unnecessary obstacles and make it effortless to step into the version of yourself you're striving to become.

This isn't about grand, overwhelming changes; it's about small, thoughtful shifts that add up over time. A home that nurtures you makes self-care second nature, helps you stay focused on what matters and gives you the space to dream bigger. Every object you choose to keep, every system you put in place, every corner you create with love – it all builds momentum towards the life you're manifesting.

As you move forward, ask yourself: is my home working for me or against me? And if it's not yet fully aligned with my vision, what's one small thing I can do today to change that? Because the little things, done consistently, are what lead to the biggest transformations.

One of the most powerful ways to start creating a home that truly supports you is by letting go of what no longer serves you. Clutter – both physical and mental – drains your energy, scatters your focus and holds you back from stepping fully into the life you want. When you clear your space, you clear your mind. In the next chapter, we're going to dive into how decluttering can bring clarity, focus and an undeniable shift in energy, making it easier than ever to manifest your dreams.

Chapter 5
SPACE TO MANIFEST

'In order to manifest anything into your life, you simply *must* create the space for it first.'

I simply cannot talk about the impact of your environment on your life and goals without also talking about the power of regular, ruthless decluttering. When I say decluttering, I don't just mean the old make-up spilling out of your bathroom cabinet or the piles of toys filling the sitting room. I totally *do* mean those things, but I also mean emotional, mental and time clutter – anything that is taking up your life and preventing you from spending time and energy on what you truly desire.

Today more than ever we have jam-packed, full-to-the-brim lives. With so many household items, clothes and toys being mass produced for a monetary price that is a fraction of the true cost to the environment, we buy every day with one-click checkout, next-day delivery and without a second's thought. Not only that, we seem to cram our diaries with more, more, more. More birthday parties, more Santa visits, more 'once in a lifetime' experiences that seem to be more 'once a year', just . . . *more!* One thing I know to be true is that if you want to *add* anything to an already full life, you will fail. In order to manifest anything into your life – whether that is a person, a business, a fun friendship circle, a second home, a new baby, whatever it is – you simply *must* create the space for it first.

You may have heard that the Universe loves a vacuum and I've found this to be true when manifesting in my own life, time and time again. Virtually as soon as I take the physical action of decluttering in whatever area of my life it is I am focusing on, I feel an instant change in my mindset as well as see quick results in my life.

There are many examples of when the Universe will fill a vacuum. If you have three days to complete a simple job, it will take three days. If you suddenly have a little extra time to yourself because the children start school, that time is soon filled and you find yourself as time-poor as before. My favourite is when you get a pay rise and you imagine what you will spend this extra money on, or even have plans to save it. Then, what happens? The vacuum swallows it up and you feel your bank balance return to the same as it was before the pay rise. On the other hand, when we create a vacuum, in space or time or energy anywhere in our lives, and we are intentional and conscious about what we want to fill that space with – magic happens.

So what does clutter in your full life actually look like?

- Your childhood friend who you feel obligated to spend time with, but who always leaves you feeling flat.
- An after-work drinking culture every Friday night that leaves you feeling drained and hungover all weekend.
- A spare room full of junk that will 'one day' be the new baby's room.
- A co-parent who you have no boundaries with and who drains you with endless messages and calls.
- A bedroom that's a catch-all for the household laundry piles, redundant exercise equipment and kids' stuff.

- A yearly girls' holiday with a friendship group who gossip and make you feel bad about yourself.
- Thousands of pounds of photography equipment for the photography business you never got off the ground.
- A stuffed-full bathroom cabinet full of toxic and expired products that you don't get on with.
- A baby ballet class at 9am on your only day to have a slow morning that the children go wild in and stresses you out.
- A garage full of junk, old boxes and clutter.

So, as you can see, there can be a wide range of 'clutter' in our lives that fills our homes and calendars, and drains the fucking life out of us. Let's take a look at how each one stops you from fulfilling your goals and living your dream life.

Your childhood friend who you feel obligated to spend time with

We all have old friendships we hang on to because we feel obligated, pressured or simply nostalgic for a time and friendship that's passed. But it's totally OK to outgrow friends or to simply drift apart due to location or life circumstances.

Motherhood is savage and we change so much because of it. Most of us have little child-free time to spend with friends and so the quality of those friendships is so important. When I was in my twenties and early thirties, I had a go-to party friend who was always up for a night on the town. We went out most weeks without fail. It was always me organising the nights out, it was always back to mine for afters or pre-drinks; it was always me. Once I got pregnant with Bohemia, I came to a startling realisation: I didn't like spending time with that friend when I was sober. I actually found the conversation so dull and she rarely, if ever, took the initiative to plan time together. I felt totally responsible that I had carried on a friendship for *years* always under the influence and that I had no idea about the real her. I felt bad, but it was the truth. Our friendship simply didn't fit into my new phase of life as a mother-to-be.

I know it can be difficult to let go of friends, especially if you don't have new ones to fill your heart with yet, but here's the thing: often you won't have the space for somebody new to come in until you create a gap in your life. As you read this passage, is there a person or a group that comes to mind that just aren't your vibe? Could you commit to lovingly releasing them so that you might make space for an incredible new friendship in your life?

One of my first ever podcast guests was *Love Island*'s Amy Hart who famously got dumped by Curtis and was perpetually single. As we were talking, she revealed her plans to freeze her eggs as she had been single for so long. She said that she was so happy to be single as her life was incredibly full with work, friends and commitments that took up all of her time. There and then I could see that she was using 'busyness' to avoid the pain of not meeting her match, and I suggested that she create as much space in her life as she could. I proposed that she create more downtime, say no to invitations and allow the space to let someone in. After only four weeks of doing this, she met the love of her life – her future husband and baby daddy all rolled into one. Talk about fast results!

An after-work drinking culture that leaves you drained and hungover

As I get older, I'm learning one thing: a Friday night out doesn't just take up the Friday night. It will often command my Saturday and even the Sunday too as I recover. Before I start sounding like Pete Doherty on a three-day bender, what I mean is your girl's forty and it legitimately takes me two full business days to recover. Now, as a single mum who doesn't get out very often, I like to go big when I do, because of precisely that – it's not very often. However, if it's every single weekend that's being affected, it might be time to ask yourself, what else could I do with that precious time? As we already know, we only have so much time and energy, and if yours is being used up on the wrong people, events or situations, it leaves nothing for you to curate your dream life! One of the reasons I was so grateful to the lockdown was that it took away so many of my options. If you think about it, motherhood can feel much the same! What can you avoid, even if just for a period of time so that you can throw yourself into Project You?

A spare room full of junk and clutter

I love to talk to women about manifesting babies and some-thing I always suggest is to clear space for the baby. Often people are squished in and don't have the room for a/another baby, but will 'cross that bridge when they come to it'. I find it very powerful to declutter with intention and begin to make that space for the soul you are calling in. With every item you donate or throw away, visualise your future baby getting closer and closer. You are sending out a powerful message to the Universe as you physically create the space. I often dream of moving back to London or even overseas, and I know that if ever I wanted to make it a serious option, the first thing I would do is start getting rid of items from my house. Maybe that's why I haven't done it yet – I'm still unsure!

The spare room isn't just a spare room, and the clutter isn't just clutter – it's what it represents. What could that spare room be if it were clear? Could it be a space for your new business venture to thrive, a place to hone an art or a guest room so family or friends could finally visit and start making memories? Only you know.

A co-parent who drains you

It's incredible how much time and emotional energy can be sapped from our lives by not having proper boundaries with our co-parents. If you are not co-parenting, this can still apply to anyone you have in your life who feels they can contact you at all times with no restrictions.

It has taken me more years than I care to admit to put in place the proper boundaries needed to communicate with my exes successfully. I used to receive streams and streams of messages, one after the other, that I felt all required responding to, justifying, explaining and correcting. These days, I simply don't. If it isn't urgent, I shan't be replying during my work time or on a rare night out. If it isn't relevant to our co-parenting relationship (for example, threats, accusations or comments on my life, looks or personality), then it simply doesn't warrant a response. It took a while for me to build that muscle of recognising that something doesn't need a response or correcting, but it is *vital* for us to learn if we are going to protect our energy and time.

One particular ex of mine would wait until I was child-free (so, very precious time I use to see friends or work), then bombard me with unsolicited opinions on my life. If I got into a communication with him, rather than settling it, it would simply fuel the fire. Before I knew it, my nervous system was shot to pieces and my energy for the day drained.

Imagine if you set some boundaries around your time and energy, especially who has access to you and when – what else could fill that space?

A bedroom that's a catch-all

A woman's bedroom should be her sanctuary from the world, but, in reality, for many mothers, it's a space that is invaded by so much stuff that simply isn't ours. A little while ago, I was reading a fascinating book about divine feminine energy – *The Goddess Path* by Kirsty Gallagher. As someone who identifies as being massively in her masculine energy (basically, don't help me – I can do it all alone; what a single mum trauma response) as well as a co-sleeper, I realised that I had no place within the walls of my home that was truly mine to go to rest, retreat and restore. OK, I had my home office which the girls didn't go into, but it wasn't a place to relax – it was to hustle! I realised that to embrace my feminine energy more, I had to create a cosy nest for the MVP of our household – *me*! I had to start enforcing some boundaries which looked like letting the girls come in to sleep, but leaving any toys in their own rooms. I don't want that shit in my space! It looked like letting the washing piles be in the laundry room, not on my floor. I cleared out everything that wasn't mine and didn't help me rest and relax. I added bed-side tables to hold all the things I needed to have a VIP sleep: magnesium for my feet, a relaxing pillow spray, lip balm – all the necessities. I curated a small collection of fiction books that had absolutely nothing to do with my work in self-development. I put down a soft bath mat in front of the mirror in my bathroom and filled my bathroom cabinet with only the products I used each day, nothing else.

I upgraded my bed in every way possible too. This is actually something I did after reading *Get Rich, Lucky Bitch!* by Denise Duffield-Thomas. In it, she says to upgrade areas of your life and home that will make you feel like a Wealthy Woman every day, such as your underwear or bed. In the past, I think I had got these upgrades a bit wrong – buying a designer bag which wasn't big enough for the compulsory nappies and wipes, and so was rarely used, or a beautiful dress that was not going to be the dress code for anywhere I was about to go. I set about creating the most premium bedtime experience possible, replacing my mattress, adding a cloud-like topper, having a pillow consultation to find the perfect pillow and upgrading my sheets to the highest thread count possible. Because life is too short to sleep on low thread count.

I winced as I saw the price of the investment in simple bed sheets, but Lord above, I use them every night! You had better believe, even years later, I *still* get into my bed and think 'what a time to be asleep'. When you create a cosy, beautiful nest, you allow yourself to be worthy of rest, to be worthy of something that is sacred and to call your own.

A yearly holiday with friends who make you feel bad about yourself

I holidayed with my girl group of friends from school every year from around the age of 16 until our mid-twenties. I want to clarify now that they didn't gossip or make me feel bad about myself, but our holiday values were definitely not aligned. As we got older, I found that what we wanted from a holiday was very different. I remember one of the last trips we took was to Cuba and I was so excited! We had planned a three-week tour of Thailand with loads of different experiences, but the morning we were due to leave, there was an attack on Bangkok airport and the whole shebang was cancelled! Cuba was our next best option. I was going hoping for fun, experiences and local culture. My friends (who I love dearly) simply wanted to sunbathe and go to bed early. I got speaking to one of the waiters who said he would take us out that night to experience the city and I couldn't believe it when the girls wouldn't leave the resort. We stopped taking annual holidays together after that. It only took one or two summers for me to meet two Americans on a night out in London who I felt an instant connection with and who invited me just one week later to backpack around Europe with them for six weeks. I said yes. I said yes because I had the time and space (and probably money!) to go because I had said no to the holidays that no longer felt in alignment. I went with them and had what was one of the most epic periods of my lifetime. Ever since, we meet up around the world and spend time in a new place having the *best* time! We've done Australia, New Orleans, New York, Mexico, Napa Valley and, at the time of writing, have just spent my 40th birthday together in the Bahamas. That's what happens when you lovingly release trips that no longer align – you find tribes who do.

Thousands of pounds of equipment for your business you never got off the ground

We've all done it – we've come up with a 'great' business idea while on maternity leave. Is it the fight against the *Peppa Pig* brain rot, is it the frantic urge to want to stay with your baby far beyond the statutory maternity leave your company gives you? Maybe it's both. But now you have a corner full of stock, equipment or whatever that isn't used. You have two options with this one. Option one is that you didn't give the business a proper shot and now is the time to really give it a go. The second option is that you hastily bought everything you needed for this new hobby/passion/business, but quickly realised that buying all the stuff is a very different hobby to actually using it. (I have a feeling that we love the purchasing process when we imagine we are going to set up a new business or start a new hobby more than the practice itself!)

I went to St Martin's College in London to study and learn how to properly use my camera (no brag, but also a brag). I used to *love* curating beautiful, ethereal outfits for Bohemia, who was a baby at the time and had absolutely no say in how often she wore a flower crown. I would fervently location-hunt for mossy hills, leafy woods or patches of wildflowers and take the loveliest pictures of her. The results were gorgeous, even if I do say so myself, and my Facebook comments were wild with other mums saying I should do it as a business. And so I did. I got a couple of my local mum friends to bring their babies to the woods under strict instructions to *not* dress them in anything with a print, bold colour or hideous cartoon pictures on them. The results were good, but I quickly realised something: I hated taking pictures of other people's children. What was a passion and a joy for me to do with my own daughter was an absolute ball-ache with young children who wouldn't sit down, stay still or look in the right direction. No thanks, not for me.

I decided to sell the majority of the photography equipment I had bought as I knew it was never going to be something I would pursue. If you have equipment or supplies lying around from business ideas or hobbies that never left the ground, it will make you feel like shit:

- 'Why did I waste so much money on that stuff that I never use?'
- 'Why do I start things then never finish them?'
- 'I can't get rid of it, it cost me so much money.'
- 'I really wish I was the kind of person who could stick to something.'

You get the vibe and it's not a vibe. If you know you don't want to continue the photography, pole dancing, candle-making, whatever it is, seeing it all sitting there will only make you feel bad about it over and over again. Sell it for what you can and move on so that you can try something new that *will* suit you!

That's not to say that you shouldn't try out lots of things – that's totally OK and is how we know what works and what doesn't. In the process of building my business, I have had *many* side hustles/businesses that have and haven't worked. Without trying, I wouldn't have got to where I am today.

To make you feel better, here are a list of my businesses/hobbies and whether they worked:

- Chihuahua clothing and accessories. This business was fabulous and I made a good income for about three years, then decided that e-commerce was not for me.
- Jewellery stamping. I had the idea to stamp bracelets with affirmations and call it 'Gratitude Rocks'. I bought the *entire* kit from Etsy for about £2,000 and, after one attempt, thought 'never again'. I sold the kit for a fraction of the price.
- Flower bikinis. After one episode of *TOWIE* showing girls in bikinis with faux flowers on them, I got on the first bus to Dalston market and purchased ten bikinis and an armload of flowers. I sat night after night sewing them on individually, but it was too labour-intensive and I gave up after a week.
- Spray-tanning. I got a kit and a one-day training course for my birthday for £100 and it quickly became my full-time job. I even got my own salon in London and won Tanning Salon of the Year two years running.
- Lash technician. I bought the kit and was trained by a random Russian lady in my spare bedroom, which,

looking back, was odd, but it worked. I did it for several years and really enjoyed it. Doing lashes was what enabled me to finally quit my nine-to-five job.

- Lash supplier. I found some amazing lashes wholesale and thought I would become a supplier, not just a technician. I bought hundreds of boxes and I hate to say, they are still in my garage as I sometimes dream about doing a couple of local clients one morning a week when the girls are at school. I miss it so much!

- Pole dancing. I took up pole dancing after reading a book on fun and I loved it! I got a bit too excited and ordered a pole for my house which was three metres tall and took up half my kitchen. I hated it! I used it once then sold it on Facebook Marketplace for half the price.

As you can see, some businesses/hobbies worked and others didn't. What's important is to part with everything that no longer aligns with your future and your dream life. Get rid of it and create the space to try something new.

A stuffed-full bathroom cabinet

Not being able to part with old products which are out of date or don't suit your skin is something to look into with money mindset work. Do you not get rid of items from your home that don't work for you because they cost a lot of money? Not being able to release stuff because of the cost is a bad money-mindset move. It maybe means that you don't think you can afford to buy them again. Being able to lovingly release them to charity or friends is a great move.

I know it can be frustrating to invest in products which claim to work wonders, and then do nothing, but them sitting in your bathroom and clogging up your precious space is tragic. So many food banks now take lightly used or new products for women's refuges and it gets them out of your hair. Rather than purchasing 1,000 wonder products, invest in a one-off consultation with a skin coach who guarantees results. I did this years ago and now have a simple three-step skincare routine and only three products in my skincare arsenal.

When you have fully stuffed cupboards and shelves of things you don't use, you can't see the items you really want and need. Since decluttering my bathroom and skincare category, my self-care has improved massively. I have few products which I know work; I can see them, I can access them and I get the results I want. Make your beauty goals easy and declutter your bathroom today.

A baby ballet class on your only day to have a slow morning

OK, now this is a big one. I used to look around at other children my girls' age and feel like they had to partake in every extra-curricular activity too. One friend's child had performed in many dance shows, another's could swim the English Channel at the age of six in a straitjacket . . . OK, not quite, but you get the vibe.

I signed up Bohemia to dancing with her friend and she finally reached the top of the village Brownies waiting list at the same time. And guess what? Of course, they were on the same night. She was in her first year of school and my twins were little babies. We would rush straight from school and get changed in the toilets of the fast-food restaurant next to the dance school. There used to be a lady who worked there who would unlock the disabled toilet for me so I could push my big double pram in there and get Bohemia changed. I later found out the lady's daughter was a single mum too and I think she felt for me when she saw me struggling. I would then walk around the shops for an hour while Bohemia danced, then it was a rush to get to Brownies 15 minutes later. She would be getting changed in the car like Mariah Carey at an awards show, then it was straight into the next activity. Meanwhile, the babies and I would get settled at home only to have to go out again at *seven o'clock* on a *school night* to collect her.

It turns out it was raising my stress levels sky high and Bohemia didn't even enjoy it. It was too much for her and she gave up. Since then, I have adopted the motto of my friend Susie Moore: let it be easy.

- Is the class at 9am on your only slow morning? Forget it.
- Is the class all the way across town, straight after school, making your drive there look like a high-speed car chase? Forget it.
- Do your children wreak havoc in the baby ballet class and give you a panic attack each time you go? Forget it.

I truly believe that in letting go of these classes which do not work for us, we will find the sports, passions and classes that they thrive in. Bohemia has since taken up and loves Irish dancing for example. Who knew?!

A garage full of junk, old boxes and clutter

Your garage, if you have one – or that spare room or cupboard – is a space which could be so many things. For me, my garage is a space that supports the kind of outdoors lifestyle I want to enjoy in the summer. It is filled with items which make my garden comfortable and hospitable all summer long. Whether it's pool chemicals and floats, sofa cushions, gas bottles, parasols or the children's outdoor toys and ride-ons, this space has been curated and organised to support me living my best hot-girl summer life. Is your garage a space filled with junk you can't fit in your house? Or is it filled with items you need to have the best summer ever? Do you have bikes for family rides or a paddling pool and sprinkler for those heatwave days? Is your spare room a graveyard of old shit nobody needs anymore but can't be bothered to take to the tip? Is the spare bedroom not fit for a guest because the priority is given to junk rather than a loved one coming to stay?

There are certain rooms of my house which I weirdly (and Frenchly?) consider male, like they are helping me have the best home life ever, and the garage is definitely one of them. It really helps me and my family set up the perfect summer spot for entertaining in our garden. I also like to store all my seasonal decorations here as I *love* to decorate my front porch for Easter (I have two large bunnies that adorn the step), Halloween (a million pumpkins and skeletons) and Christmas (hello five-foot nutcrackers!).

Is it possible that your garage/spare room/cupboard could have an alternative use? I often dream of turning my garage into a beauty salon where I could do lashes or into a little self-contained unit where friends or family could stay. I'm lucky enough to have a spare bedroom now (I've never had one before!) and it could very easily get filled with junk! I must admit, there are times when excess books and work stuff begin to creep out of my office into there and I have to check myself. That room gives me the gift of hosting. I'm a London girl turned country bumpkin and I want my friends to come and visit me. That room enables them to have a comfortable stay and for me to reconnect with my loved ones. It also transforms from September to December into a top-secret gift room! My daughters know it's a no-go area and it becomes my safe space to store all the magic of Christmas.

If your space is filled with random shit you don't need, what dream could take its place? A home office, a home salon, a holiday let? The only way to find out is to declutter and see . . .

I hope this chapter helps you to see that in an already jam-packed life, it can feel impossible to magnetise more. Remember, if you always find yourself saying, 'I have no time', 'I'm so busy' or 'I'd love to have the space to . . .', then the Universe will agree with you that you don't have the capacity.

The easiest and simplest way to intentionally bring more abundance into your life is to regularly and ruthlessly declutter everything that takes up space in your home, your mind, your life and your calendar.

Now, I love a declutter as much as Stacey Solomon, but unless you set fire to your entire house – including the piles of laundry – there will *always* be chores for us to do as we run our lives, our children's lives and our homes. That, my friend, is unavoidable. So, how do you turn your to-do list into chore therapy? Let's find out.

Chapter 6

'This simple shift is going to turn your to-do list into a selection of self-care rituals to nourish you.'

With the risk of sounding like a 1950s' housewife, we must face the honest truth: even here in the glorious 2020s, it is mostly women who bear the majority of unpaid labour. Whether that is childcare, housework or the invisible load, we must admit it still exists.

Yes, there will be the exceptions to the rule, but, as a mother who has many other mothers in her life, it is *us* who have a downpour of unpaid tasks raining down on us daily. These are, of course, necessary, but if we're honest, they do take us away from working on our bigger goals and dreams. Because that's just a fact, right? As we touched on in Chapter 1, manifesting isn't just about wishing and hoping – it's about action. And action takes time and energy.

I had a dream of writing a book about manifesting for mothers – and me aligning with it, visualising it and embodying it got the wonderful Penguin Random House to offer me this incredible opportunity to write this very book . . . but that wasn't the end of it. I then had to find the time to actually write it! I am currently writing this chapter at 5am in the darkness of my bedroom, typing as quietly as I can next to my sleeping daughter. Tonight, I will forgo a Netflix marathon and write into the night. Later this week, I will sneak my laptop into soft play and try to get some more writing in while my twins play. I *have* to create the time and space in my life to make this dream happen, and that will come at a cost. Something has to give.

Redress the balance

We only have so much to give in a day and I just couldn't begin this chapter on chore therapy (which is magical, by the way) without addressing the imbalance that still occurs in most households. If you are in a partnership or a marriage, I highly recommend some simple steps to remedy an imbalance if you identify one. I would suggest a weekly meeting with your partner, ideally on a Sunday night, to plan out your week and organise your household and family – much like a business. Make a list of all the weekly household responsibilities and use two different highlighters to mark who is responsible for what. This simple task, especially if you are both working, should high-light the imbalance.

Redress the balance and decide what is fair for you both. Remember, it's not just the physical tasks, but the invisible load too. The invisible load for mothers is the constant, unseen mental and emotional labour required to keep a household and family running smoothly. Unlike physical chores, this burden exists largely in the mind – anticipating needs, remembering schedules, managing emotions and ensuring everything flows seamlessly. It's the mother who keeps track of when the kids need new shoes, who remembers the birthday party gifts and who notices when the laundry detergent is running low before it becomes a problem. It's being the default parent for school emails, medical appointments and last-minute costume days. It's the weight of knowing what each child needs emotionally, ensuring they feel heard and supported, while also managing the never-ending to-do list of life. The invisible load is exhausting because it's relentless and, yet, because it's not always physically visible, it often goes unacknowledged. So, how do we resolve this?

If you can agree that each week your partner will now be responsible for three to four additional tasks that were unfairly loaded onto your plate, it's now an agreement between the two of you and they should uphold their end of the deal. It's no longer about you asking them each week to help you with 'your' tasks or you feeling overwhelmed with life – it's simply about them doing their part.

I'm the most single person you've ever met, but I've been told this weekly meeting and agreeing who is doing drop-offs, parties, shopping, cooking, cleaning, and so on, is very powerful and effective.

For those of you going it alone, I just wanted to say that no, it's not fair that everything falls to you and I see you. I know firsthand how hard it is. I feel like manifesting money is so important for all women, but specifically for single mothers. If you take the time to work on your money mindset, you will create all kinds of beautiful opportunities for you and your family. I began working on mine properly when my babies were newborns and it gave me freedom, time, energy and incredible experiences. I've just decided in this moment that this book absolutely *needs* a chapter on money mindset, so more on that later (see Chapter 12). This was simply to acknowledge that once you get your money mindset right, you can delegate a lot of daily tasks, but still, the mother load is *real*.

I'm a single mother with three young children, one of whom has terrible night terrors which can keep the entire household up all night, leaving us drained and exhausted the next day.

Another mother could look at me and say, how lucky you are! Maybe her child's father doesn't spend time with them and she is the only caregiver 24/7. Mothers of multiples will feel jealous of mothers of singletons and wonder all day what she does with her extra arm. Mothers of sick children in hospital pine for the freedom and time of mothers with healthy children. It does us no good to compare our cards, but what I do know to be true is that every single mother I know is struggling with having enough time and energy for her own goals and dreams.

Transform Your To-Do List into Self-Care Rituals

Be honest . . . how often do you find yourself saying: 'I'm so busy I have no time for self-care'? As modern-day mothers who have been told we can 'have it all' but often feel like we have to 'do it all', it can feel *impossible* to carve out a little time for our own well-being. In between the childcare, our relationships, the housework, trying to stay hydrated, keeping in contact with our friends, keeping up with work and the *billion* other responsibilities, *where* are we supposed to fit in self-care?

I discovered a simple mindset shift after reading Kirsty Gallagher's *The Goddess Path*. It absolutely transformed the way I approached my everyday tasks around the home and with my family. This simple shift is going to turn your to-do list into a selection of self-care rituals to nourish you. What I love most about this practice is that it takes no extra time or energy, is super easy and kind of delves into the art of romanticising your life, which I am a huge fan of (and which we'll cover in detail in Chapter 11).

We're going to look at a range of common motherhood tasks which I hope you relate to and how we can transform them into self-care rituals through chore therapy. 'Chore therapy' is the idea of transforming everyday household tasks into moments of mindfulness, movement and even cognitive rest. For mothers, chores can feel like an endless, thankless cycle, but shifting your perspective can turn them into something more nourishing. Instead of rushing through dishwashing or resenting the laundry, these tasks can become small rituals of presence. The rhythmic folding of clothes, the satisfaction of a freshly swept floor – when done mindfully, these chores can offer a break from mental overwhelm, allowing you to reset and re-centre.

Beyond mindfulness, household tasks also provide gentle movement that supports both physical and mental well-being – hanging laundry, vacuuming or tidying up all keep you active in small but meaningful ways. These moments also serve as cognitive breaks, giving your brain a chance to rest from decision-making and screen time. Many people find that their best ideas come while cleaning or doing repetitive tasks, as the subconscious mind gets space to process thoughts freely. By reframing chores as a therapeutic tool rather than a burden, they can become an opportunity to ground yourself, reconnect with your body, create a sense of accomplishment in even the busiest of days and open you up to the life you desire.

Embrace all physical movement

I know I have been guilty of skipping gym day for ooh . . . about 15 years running now, stating that I simply do not have the time or energy for it. Rather than that being a shit excuse, it turns out I may have been on to something. French women, widely considered to be the most chic, fit and healthy of all the world's women, have a theory: that exercise isn't so much a separate activity to fit into your day, but rather something that is a part of life.

So, what does that look like? Rather than trying to carve out the time, getting the children taken care of, jumping in the car and driving to the gym, you instead embrace all forms of physical movement the day throws at you: take the stairs rather than the escalator; walk to school, don't drive; carry the shopping like it's a set of weights; give the dog an extra ten minutes on his evening walk; stretch and clean those top shelves. It all counts! Getting a simple step counter helps you see just how much activity you're doing on a daily basis and you can make it your goal to reach 10,000 steps per day. All of a sudden, all of those jobs which involved you exerting energy feel less draining and instead become a part of your daily active lifestyle plan to be embraced, not an inconvenience.

Use household tasks as daily cognitive breaks

Now what about those lower impact activities that might not exactly get the heart pumping but need doing none the less? Well, low-energy tasks, such as chopping carrots, pulling weeds and folding laundry, all help your mental health more than you can imagine. Doing something physical with your hands is linked to several mental health benefits: mindfulness and feeling present in the moment, stress reduction, boosting dopamine levels as well as activating your parasympathetic nervous system, which in turn reduces your cortisol levels.

These small tasks also give us an added benefit: when you engage in mundane, repetitive tasks with your hands, like loading the dishwasher, your brain experiences what's known as a cognitive break or passive attention shift. When you're deeply focused on something, like problem-solving or manifesting a goal, your prefrontal cortex, the part of your brain responsible for decision-making, can become overworked. Surely we've all felt that overwhelming burnout feeling? Engaging in simple tasks allows your DMN to take over, which is when your brain starts making subconscious connections and insights.

This is why mundane tasks often spark creativity and problem-solving. Have you ever noticed how great ideas come to you while you're in the shower, walking or doing something boring? That's because these activities lower cognitive load, allowing your brain to make unexpected connections. Studies show that engaging in 'mindless' activities encourages divergent thinking, which is essential for creativity.

Repetitive hand movements, like knitting or kneading dough, also activate the parasympathetic nervous system, reducing stress and promoting relaxation. It's similar to meditation in that your brain slows down, enters an alpha wave state and allows for clarity and calm.

Taking a break from focused work and engaging in a simple task helps your brain consolidate new information. You may have heard of the Pomodoro Technique which uses this. The Pomodoro Technique is a time-management method – if you don't know what it is, you should get to know it! The technique breaks work into focused 25-minute intervals, known as 'pomodoros', followed by short 5-minute breaks. This cycle is designed to maximise productivity while preventing burnout. But what many people don't realise is that those short breaks are not just about resting – they play a crucial role in how our brains process and retain information. Research shows that stepping away from a task, even for a few minutes, allows our brains to consolidate new information and strengthen memory pathways. Instead of overwhelming our cognitive load, these breaks give the mind a chance to organise and store what we've just learnt, making it easier to recall later.

During these five-minute pauses, the brain shifts from an active state of problem-solving and deep focus to a more passive mode, where it continues processing information in the background. This is when new knowledge gets integrated and connections are made between ideas. Without these breaks, the brain remains overloaded, making it harder to absorb and retain details. For mothers juggling endless to-do lists, using the Pomodoro Technique can be a game changer – not just for getting things done, but for ensuring that new information, whether it's work-related or something as simple as remembering a child's schedule, actually sticks. These tiny moments of rest, often dismissed as unimportant, are the key to working smarter, not harder. So what should we do on these five-minute breaks? Stare into the distance or close your eyes – what a treat!

This effect is also powerful for manifestation. When you're too focused on the 'how' of manifesting something, you can create mental resistance. Letting go and engaging in hands-on, repetitive tasks helps release that resistance, allowing ideas, opportunities and intuition to flow more naturally. So yes, I'm saying that folding the laundry is your meditation and washing the dishes is your brainstorming session!

This is why people so enjoy knitting, crafts and embroidery, and I guess why adult colouring books became such a huge mindfulness/mental health trend. You're able to indulge in those, too, by the way, to help you manifest. I often join my daughters for some quality time around the kitchen table as we all draw, craft and colour. I use that time to not only connect with them, but to switch off my brain and colour, draw and visualise whatever it is I want to manifest. It could be me looking fit, toned and happy on an exotic beach or my personal favourite – I used to draw and paint my dream house over and over again. That was before it became my reality. I'll speak more about crafting your vision in Chapter 8.

I remember when I lived in London with Bohemia, I used

to take her to this commune in north London, that was absolute *goals* by the way, for a Waldorf Steiner toddler group. It was wild and run by an elderly, kind, South American woman who would get all the mothers to sit and do a craft together while the children played. This was very intentional as it stopped mothers hovering over their children, interrupting their play. It was genius! She explained to me one day that back when we lived in tribes, mothers would not have been just sitting, watching their children play, the women would have all sat together weaving or doing something physical with their hands. Us sitting and needle felting a mouse was the 21st-century north London yummy mummy version of that.

When I think about the concept of the cognitive break, I feel nostalgic for my days of doing the repetitive, monotonous yet relaxing work of eyelash extensions in my London salon. These days, so much of my work involves quite complex tasks: researching, recording, editing, writing and planning. None of it is easy on the brain. I often feel overwhelmed, burnt out and lacking inspiration, but using my household tasks as daily creativity sessions or meditations is an absolute *hack*! Don't you feel different about peeling potatoes or hanging up laundry now?

Reframe the task

Imagine for a moment that you need to clean your kitchen. Firstly, the audacity – I had no idea how much of adult life would be spent cleaning a kitchen that I only just cleaned the day before. Rather than seeing this as a thankless task to be endured, approach it this way: I get to clean this beautiful space because I deserve a clean, inspirational and organised kitchen to cook meals in and enjoy the sacred ritual of mealtimes with my family. This reframe works all the time, for any job.

Imagine you have to make your bed – what a ball-ache you may think. Or you can choose to turn this into a mindful ritual in creating the ultimate sanctuary for you to reset and renew. As we discussed in the previous chapter, a woman's bedroom should be her most sacred, nurturing environment, and what better way to nurture yourself than to keep this space beautiful, clean and well-stocked with everything you need to rest. Embrace and enjoy creating a gorgeous haven for yourself.

Food shopping is one particular task which has evolved a lot for me over the years. As I touched on in Chapter 4, I've often found this difficult and I'm *still* teaching myself to meal plan and food shop to this very day. A few years ago, I did a lot of money mindset work and took it slightly too far, delegating every single household task I could, including my food shop. I ordered online once a week and it was picked, packed and delivered for me. While this is a great time- and energy-saving tip, I realised I find great pleasure in doing it myself. As I set my 'health is wealth' motto, it became important to me to become more connected to my food again, to feel and smell the produce myself, to see all that was on offer and also teach my young daughters through example how to pick out healthy food options, meal plan and create a tasty menu. Our weekly food shop on a Monday is actually one of my favourite family activities of the week now due to this mindset shift. I take my twins, list in hand, and set about filling our trolley with all the whole foods we need to create nourishing meals, family favourites and our nightly fruit and veg platters. I will read out the various fruits and vegetables we need and the girls will rush off to identify them, bringing back the best of the bunch. I adore the feeling of gathering it all and knowing it will do us such good. Food shopping *can* feel like self-care when you look at it through the lens of 'I deserve to have a kitchen full of fresh, healthy, tasty and nutritious food.'

Laundry is a job that I used to have a love/hate relationship with. I love the washing and drying, it's just the putting away that I find an absolute pain. My laundry would pile up, getting bigger and bigger until nobody had anything left to wear and I would spend the mornings frantically digging through the pile to find a clean school uniform. I saw a video online all about letting your young children help with household tasks and turning them into an activity rather than trying to keep them amused while you do it alone. Worse than that, using your precious child-free time in the evenings doing chores you hate. No thank you very much, not for me. I had experimented with letting the girls help me cook, which was usually quite stressful seeing them butcher a £3 pack of strawberries to mush, trying to cut them with their special toddler knives, but laundry wasn't something they could mess up, right? I started to let the laundry pile up until there was a good amount, then we would all go upstairs to do it together as a family. It has turned out to be Riva's absolute favourite thing to do! We work as a team, sometimes quickly and efficiently, sometimes not if I'm honest – but all having fun and working together. As I shake, fold, hang and put away the clothes, I think about how grateful I am to have a wardrobe full of clean, organised items so that I may dress for the life I want every day. I deserve to have clean piles of pyjamas in my drawer, to have my favourite outfits clean and hanging ready for my next event or socks neatly rolled for the next cold day.

Not only have you provided a free, family-bonding activity, but you're teaching your children how to live and run a home as well as caring for your future self who gets to dress for her best life. You simply cannot do this if you are scurrying around each morning looking for your favourite clothes in the dirty washing pile.

I don't know about you, but my car becomes a cesspit from hell within a few weeks of being cleaned. My daughters insist on carrying toys, books and handfuls of snacks into the car with each trip. Regularly clear out and clean your car, simply because you deserve to drive around in a pleasant environment every day. Clean the surfaces, vacuum the floor, add a fragranced essential oil diffuser and stock the central console with sunglasses, snacks and wipes along with anything else to enhance your drive. Imagine you are an Uber Lux driver trying to create the most comfortable, aspirational, luxurious experience possible for the passenger, who, spoiler alert . . . is you! Make it a premium experience to elevate your every day. Every time I think I need to upgrade my car to something more luxurious, I realise I can experience that luxury instantly with a simple clear out, clean up and restock.

As you can see from these examples, this simple mindset shift changes tasks from draining jobs which we feel rob us of our time into self-care rituals that are not only good for our bodies and minds, but are designed to elevate our daily lives. This brings me to quite an interesting point concerning creating a clean and beautiful mealtime environment . . .

Infuse love into your daily routines

Did you know that how you consume food affects its nutritional properties? In 1978, the University of Ohio conducted a study on rabbits to examine cholesterol levels and heart disease. Two groups of rabbits were fed the same high-cholesterol diet. However, after the study, it was found that one group of rabbits had significantly lower cholesterol levels and fewer signs of heart disease than the other, despite eating the exact same food. They discovered that these rabbits were being cared for by a lab assistant who regularly handled them with kindness, spoke to them gently and petted them while feeding them.

The other rabbits were clearly cared for by a heartless bastard, because they were fed without interaction and experienced the expected negative health effects. This study revealed that nurturing environments, positive interactions and emotional states can influence metabolism and overall health. So . . . does that mean a Chinese takeaway is good for me if I have a hot, loving man spoon-feed me it while I watch *Keeping Up With the Kardashians*?

This principle applies to our home environments as well. Just as the rabbits thrived in an environment of warmth and care, the way we curate and set up our kitchens and dining rooms can directly affect our well-being. If one of your goals is optimal health for you and your family, don't focus just on the food itself, but the environment in which you are preparing and consuming it. Create an eating environment that feels safe, warm and supportive by cleaning, decluttering, using soft lighting and incorporating items that bring joy – this can shift the energy and improve overall wellness.

Mindful eating is another way to apply this concept. Instead of eating while you're distracted, stressed or rushed, choosing to eat in a calm, pleasant setting can enhance digestion and nutrient absorption. Infusing love into daily routines, whether through cooking, cleaning or simply being present in your home, shifts the energy of the space and influences how we feel in it.

As we move through the year, us mothers often feel the load more around the holidays – think Easter, Halloween and Christmas. It's often down to us to create the magic, plan the traditions, wrap the gifts, bake the treats and make everything feel special. And while it can be overwhelming at times, I fully embrace it, remembering that not only am I creating a magical childhood for them, but also, in the process, I deserve a beautiful motherhood too – 'their childhood is my motherhood'.

These aren't just years I'm giving to them; they are years that shape me too. Motherhood isn't just about creating memories for our children – it's about living them ourselves. So instead of feeling burdened by the weight of making everything perfect, I remind myself that I, too, am allowed to enjoy it. I can choose traditions that light me up, let go of the pressure to do it all and be present in the beauty of the season. Because, one day, they won't remember if the table setting was Pinterest-worthy or if every detail was flawless. They'll remember how it *felt* – the warmth, the joy, the love – and I'll remember that I was right there in it with them, not just orchestrating the magic, but living it too.

Maybe I'm unorganised, maybe I have undiagnosed ADHD or maybe I'm just a mother trying to keep up with all the expectations put upon me by myself and society: expectations to earn a living, run my business, mother my children, be present and play, cook healthy meals, post a reel every day, keep the house clean, do the laundry, keep up with my skincare routine, remember to text my friends, try to have a social life and read all of the 1,000 emails I get every single day from school . . . it's enough to give you instant burnout. This is where the idea for this book originally came from – the fact that, as mothers, we know that the law of attraction works, we simply don't have the time, space or energy in our lives to be consistent with it. This is why I am so into organisation as well as time- and energy-saving hacks to create spaciousness in our homes and lives to be able to create something new for ourselves.

In the next chapter, we'll take that one step further by looking at how you can live your best life, one week at a time.

Chapter 7

MASTER YOUR WEEK, MASTER YOUR LIFE

'This isn't about cramming more onto the to-do list; it's about doing the right things at the right times, in a way that supports both your daily life and your long-term desires.'

As mothers, how often are we told to make the most of every moment? Old ladies in the supermarket will stop us with our pushchairs or trolleys full of babies and tell us to enjoy it while it lasts, as it goes far too quickly. We know that they are right – we know that these days right now are the good old days – but it's hard to feel it and enjoy it when we are meeting ourselves coming backwards. We can only really be present and enjoy these moments when we are calm, have the energy to take care of ourselves and have shit under control.

Time and energy are the most valuable resources a mother has, yet they're often the first things to feel stretched thin. Between school runs, meal planning, household tasks and work, it can feel like there's no space left for personal goals, self-care or the quiet moments needed for clarity and creativity. But what if time wasn't something to fight against, but something to intentionally design?

The key to making space for both getting things done and manifesting your goals lies in managing energy just as much as managing time. It's not just about cramming more onto the to-do list; it's about doing the right things at the right times, in a way that supports both your daily life and your long-term desires.

Very early on in my working life, I went to college to train to be a PA. I went on to be a PA for several directors of big companies. Let me tell you, organising their lives was far simpler than my job now, which came with *zero* training: running the work/school/class schedules of four people, maintaining a house and garden, organising of all the regular festivities such as Christmas, birthdays, other kids' birthdays, World Book Day, Easter, Halloween, Bonfire Night, the charity bake-a-cake sale, careers day – you name it! Along with the upkeep of everyone's medical, optical and dental appointments, buying, preparing and cooking three meals a day, making sure everyone gets play dates (including me!), problem-solving the multitude of issues that come up at any given time – from school bullying to diagnosing ADHD – *it's fucking exhausting* and should be the full-time job of about three people. It's enough to make you toss your goal list into the bin and forget all about it. But, over the past few years, I've found some incredible hacks for keeping one's shit together *and* creating the life of your dreams, and you may be surprised how simple and practical they are.

Weekly Planning

A couple of years ago, I started planning out my week on a Sunday night and it changed my goddamn life. Yes, I already had a diary, but still I would often miss appointments, be late, double-book myself and leave no space for the things that mattered.

This simple act of sitting down with my diary, phone and weekly planner on a Sunday night has become not only an essential meeting with myself to run my family and house, but also a favourite act of self-care for future me. Here's how you can incorporate this hack into your life too . . .

Mandatory appointments

Go through the upcoming week and write out every single place you need to be, even if it's obvious, like the school run. Nursery drop-offs, baby groups, dance classes, work shifts – everything that is mandatory and at a set time goes in. From there, you can see exactly what you have to do and where you have to be on any given day.

Flexibility is key here. No two days are the same when you have children, and trying to stick to rigid plans often leads to frustration. Instead of striving for perfect routines, create adaptable structures: time-blocking loosely, batch-working tasks and allowing for the natural ebb and flow of energy throughout the day. Time-blocking might look like dedicating your baby's afternoon nap to working on business ideas or health goals. Batching tasks is simply doing all similar jobs together, such as dedicating a morning to listing all your Vinted items at once or, if your job requires a social media presence, recording your reels or preparing a month of posts in one sitting.

Some mornings might be perfect for tackling deep work or personal projects, while others are best suited for rest, reflection or simply being present. The goal is to move in harmony with your energy rather than forcing productivity for productivity's sake.

Semi-rigid appointments

From here, I have built a little routine of including semi-structured events in my schedule. They are activities which are not set in stone, but by putting them in at the same time each week, I end up doing them on autopilot, and therefore they become effortless. I highly recommend setting up weekly semi-rigid appointments if you find yourself going back and forth trying to arrange catch-ups with friends and family. I used to go weeks at a time without seeing my friend Suzy – we were the last of our friends to have babies at home, with all the rest being off at school. In a bid to reduce the mental load and the back and forth of 'I haven't seen you for ages' or 'We really should meet up soon', I simply invited her and her son to a weekly church baby group in my village that my girls loved. I told Suzy that I was there every Wednesday, rain or shine, and, as a result, I now spend time with my friend almost every week. It's become a fixture in our weekly diaries that requires no communication or arranging. I love it.

Meal planning

When I say 'meal planning', please don't imagine I'm up at midnight meal-prepping and freezing vegan meals a month in advance – oh no. I simply mean to plan what to eat in a given week, giving yourself the space to eat out or get a food delivery when you want or need to. I find planning my meals in advance and putting them in my diary has helped me achieve so many goals, from saving money to eating healthier. It seems such a 1950s thing to do – our mothers and grandmothers had specific nights: Monday was steak night; Friday was fish night – but maybe they were on to something and we can learn from the mothers of the past.

I meal plan for the week so that I can successfully food shop on the Monday and stick to my health goals. Doing this eases my decision fatigue which can drain me. Decision fatigue is the silent energy drain that most mothers don't even realise is weighing them down. From choosing what to cook for dinner, coordinating school schedules and remembering every little detail of family life, the sheer number of daily decisions can leave you mentally exhausted before you even have a moment to think about your own goals and dreams. High achievers like Steve Jobs famously eliminated trivial choices; for example, by wearing the same outfit every day so he could preserve his mental energy for what truly mattered (to him). While we might not all want to adopt a black turtleneck uniform, by reducing the number of small, repetitive decisions we make each day, we free up space for the bigger, life-changing choices – the ones that move us toward our desires, rather than just keeping us afloat.

Once I've put the mandatory events, semi-rigid events and meal planning into my diary, I can see the spaces left. This is where I get to decide what is important to me that might otherwise get dumped in the busyness of mum life. It could be having a self-care evening, setting time aside to start a side hustle, writing a chapter of this book, giving my eldest daughter some much-needed one-on-one time or making sure I do a workout three times a week. When it's planned and scheduled in, I know it is far more likely to happen.

The Art of Juggling

Life as a mother often feels like an endless juggling act – with family, work, relationships, self-care and the countless responsibilities that make up daily life. But not all balls are created equal. Some are made of glass – they are fragile, precious and irreplaceable – and others are made of plastic, so they are important but resilient. It's only when I came across this analogy by bestselling author Nora Roberts that I changed how I feel when I occasionally 'drop the ball'. If you drop a glass ball, it smashes. It *may* be able to be fixed, but it's difficult and may never be the same again. Plastic balls, on the other hand, will bounce. The wisdom lies in knowing which is which, because trying to keep every ball in the air at all times is not only exhausting but impossible. This brings me on to prioritisation – an *essential* skill for the manifesting mother.

The importance of prioritisation

Did you know that the word 'priority' comes from the Latin 'prior', meaning 'first'? So, technically, it's impossible to have more than one priority, but I bet the old man who created Latin had no idea we 21st-century mamas would be caring for our children and striving for achievements in our own lives too! I fully allow myself to have more than one priority.

The art of prioritisation is not about doing more, it's about doing what matters most. True balance doesn't come from cramming more into the day; it comes from clarity – knowing what deserves your time and energy and what can wait.

Going back to the ball analogy, glass balls represent the things that truly matter – the well-being of our children, our health, our deepest relationships and the core values that shape our lives. In more practical terms, they are getting a child to school on time each morning, turning up to work or being there for a friend who really needs us. If a glass ball is dropped, it can crack or even break beyond repair. Neglecting our health, for example, may lead to burnout or illness. Failing to nurture our closest relationships can create a distance that's hard to bridge. These are the areas that require the most care, attention and protection. They may not always demand urgency, but they hold the deepest significance.

Plastic balls are the things that feel important in the moment, but can actually be set down without lasting damage. The perfect home, the never-ending to-do list, the pressure to be everything to everyone, getting the car cleaned . . . these things can be paused, adjusted or even let go. A missed school bake sale, an unanswered email or a slightly messy house won't derail your life or define your worth. But the energy spent obsessing over them can take away from what truly matters.

The challenge for mothers is recognising which balls are glass and which are plastic in any given season. What may be a glass ball one year – perhaps a demanding career move or an ageing parent – may shift into a plastic one later, or vice versa. This means continually reassessing your priorities with compassion and clarity, and giving yourself permission to let go of perfection and understanding that dropping a plastic ball is not failure; it's wisdom.

At the heart of this philosophy is the idea that balance isn't about doing everything – it's about doing what matters most. It's about releasing the guilt that comes from letting go of the unnecessary and embracing the peace that comes with protecting what's truly valuable. The art of juggling isn't in keeping every ball in the air, but in knowing which ones to catch and which ones to let bounce.

One of the biggest challenges for mothers is distinguishing between what is truly important and what simply feels urgent. Many days are filled with little fires to put out – laundry piles, unexpected errands and endless decision-making – but the things that genuinely move life forward often get pushed aside. A heartfelt conversation with your child, time to rest and recharge, or space to pursue a personal dream often don't demand immediate attention, but they are the very things that shape a fulfilling life. Without conscious prioritisation, the loudest tasks will always overshadow the most important ones.

To break this cycle, carve out time each week to decide what matters most. What are the three most important things that need your energy? What small step can you take towards a long-term dream? By setting these priorities first, you ensure that life isn't just happening to you, but you're creating it with intention.

Switch up your language

Do you find yourself often saying, 'Sorry, I didn't have time'? I cringe every time I hear myself say it, and so I made a promise to myself to change the language I use. I no longer say, 'I didn't have time', instead I simply say, 'I didn't prioritise it.' Doesn't that feel less frantic? More true? Prioritisation is not just a skill we can learn to master; it's a form of self-care, a way to ensure that your life is being shaped by intention rather than urgency.

It's also important to learn to let go of the guilt that comes with saying no. Mothers are often conditioned to believe they should handle everything flawlessly, but the truth is, something will always have to give. The most successful people in the world don't try to do everything; they focus on what moves them forward. This means letting go of the pressure to be constantly available, delegating where possible and recognising that some things – like a perfectly clean house or replying to messages instantly – are simply not essential.

And then there's the part that so many mothers neglect: self-care as a non-negotiable – not as a luxury, not as something to squeeze in when everything else is done, but as a necessary part of being a thriving, powerful woman. When a mother is exhausted, overwhelmed and running on empty, everything else suffers. I saw a viral reel on Instagram that talked about how the number-one factor for a child thriving was the quality of the mother's happiness. I know from personal experience, and I'm sure you do too, that when my cup is empty, I have nothing to give to my daughters. I can get snappy, be sad and have no energy. While that's normal and OK every now and then (basically every time I have a period – see Chapter 3 for why!), I don't want that to be the version of their mother that my children recognise. Taking time for yourself – whether that's working on a business, seeing friends, spending time child-free, going on a date or having an adults-only holiday – is not selfish; it's what allows you to show up as your best self for the people you love. When you prioritise moments for yourself, you're not just refuelling, you're reinforcing the belief that your goals, dreams and well-being matter. Remember, the more you value yourself and treat yourself well, the more you believe you deserve in life and the more you allow yourself to manifest.

Ultimately, mastering the art of prioritisation means making peace with imperfection. Some days, the to-do list will remain unfinished, and that's OK. What matters is that the things that truly deserve your time – your health, your relationships, your passions – are not consistently sacrificed for things that don't. The goal is not to do everything; the goal is to do what matters most and to trust that by focusing on what truly counts, everything else will fall into place.

What would you like to add to your weekly schedule that is important and vital to you reaching your goals, but always seems to get forgotten about? Is it one night a week to see friends child-free? Is it a workout class you could commit to? Ask yourself now: what is the one activity you could add to your weekly schedule as a non-negotiable? How do you make it happen? Do you need to speak to your partner, your co-parent or maybe your family and ask them to help out? Doing this may be uncomfortable, but asking once is going to see you receive the benefit with a compound result.

Let me show you what I mean here using two scenarios:

1. Ask once, receive once: You're burnt out, haven't seen your friends in forever and need something for yourself. You say to your partner you need a night with friends and you go. You have a fab time, but it only seems to highlight to you how much you need this. You think about asking again in a few weeks, but you feel bad and the weeks just seem to slip by with messages from your friends saying, 'It's been ages, we must do it again!'

2. Ask once, compound benefit: You're burnt out, unfit and you desperately need something for yourself in the midst of the preschool years. You sit down with your partner, mum, babysitter, whoever you need to get on board, and explain that you are feeling overwhelmed by constant mothering and that you need something once a week that's just for you. It could simply be a local women's circle, an exercise class or a weekly dinner date with a friend – it really doesn't matter. They see from your weekly schedule how constant it is and agree to support you. At this point, you book that shit in as a recurring appointment so that it becomes automatic, expected. As the weeks go by, you begin to see the effects of taking that little time for yourself and it elevates other areas of your life. Boom!

But what if there *isn't* any room for these necessities? What if we are overscheduled, overbooked, overworked and burnt out? Something's got to change. Enter the incredible 4D Method, which I discovered while reading *Working Hard, Hardly Working* by the incredible Grace Beverley.

The 4D Method

The 4D Method, aka the Eisenhower or Urgent-Important Matrix, is a time-management tool that helps you prioritise tasks based on their urgency and importance. It was popularised by former US President Dwight D. Eisenhower, who famously said, 'What is important is seldom urgent, and what is urgent is seldom important.' *How bloody true is this*? Really think about that. We get caught up in years and years of minutiae and delay doing the things that will change our lives. Well, not any more!

The matrix divides tasks into four categories:

1. Urgent and Important (Do): These are tasks that require immediate attention and are crucial for your long-term goals, such as dealing with emergencies or pressing deadlines.
2. Not Urgent but Important (Defer): These tasks are important for your personal growth and success, but don't need immediate action. Examples include planning, strategising or focusing on self-care.
3. Urgent but Not Important (Delegate): These tasks demand quick action, but don't directly contribute to your long-term objectives. They could be things that someone else can do, like answering non-urgent emails or handling routine requests.
4. Not Urgent and Not Important (Ditch): These are tasks that are neither urgent nor important, such as mindlessly scrolling through social media or engaging in distractions. These should be minimised or eliminated from your schedule altogether.

For busy mothers, especially those juggling work, home life and self-care, the Eisenhower Matrix provides a simple framework to assess and focus on what truly matters. By spending more time on important tasks (like bonding with your children, advancing your career or self-care) and eliminating distractions or delegating low-priority tasks, you can create a more balanced and fulfilling life. The matrix helps break down overwhelming to-do lists and enables you to move through your day with intention and clarity.

We all have a massive to-do list at any given time, right? So, when planning your week, use the 4D Method to avoid overwhelm, create space and stay in alignment with your goals.

Ditch it

As you look through your schedule or to-do list, is there anything you could simply ditch? We often repeat stuff on autopilot and we sometimes need to ask ourselves if that commitment, class or job is still serving us. That particular toddler group that is overstimulating, overpriced and sends your toddler into a meltdown every week? Don't sweat it, ditch it! Ask yourself: *Does this truly need to be done or am I just doing it out of habit, guilt or obligation?*

Delegate it

We've been told we can have it all, but it doesn't mean we need to *do* it all. Look through the running of your family and house for the coming week and ask your partner, if you have one, if there's anything they can take off your hands. Perhaps you could assign age-appropriate jobs to the children, ask your partner to take over certain tasks or outsource things like cleaning, laundry or food shopping (get it delivered). If I have a particularly busy week and I need a break on meal planning, for example, I sometimes get a meal kit delivery service, taking away the job of food shopping and meal planning in one!

Defer it

Some weeks are busier than others and there is only so much we can do. Prioritise what is important that week – for example, if you're hosting a kids' birthday party, you would want the house and garden to look good and have time to get your hair blow-dried, but it's not important if your car or bedroom is a mess. Defer anything that's not important, not time-sensitive or both.

Do it

If it's on your list and it's both important and is going to move you closer to your goals, whatever they may be, do it now and do it with intention.

Using this 4D Method helps time- and energy-poor mothers focus on what matters and what's urgent in all areas of life while creating the space to change their lives longer term. Time isn't just about scheduling; it's about designing a life where both responsibilities and desires coexist. When you begin managing your energy wisely, simplifying where possible and building flexibility into your days, you create the space not only to keep up with life, but to shape it in the way you truly want.

The Power of Focus

We have already talked about how we mothers don't have enough time or energy in the day for all the demands and so we have to focus on what is going to improve our lives with needlepoint precision.

Years ago, I was a guest on a podcast and the host said that the most important goal to work on in your life is the one that is going to change your life the most dramatically and will make many of your other goals materialise a lot more easily. I have a couple of examples of how laser focus has propelled me forward in a short space of time and I hope it inspires you.

Laser focus 1

When Bohemia and I moved into that one-bedroom flat above the noisy pub in north London, I was very aware that this era of our lives wouldn't be forever and I embraced it. However, I won't lie, it wasn't easy, nor was it the life I wanted my daughter to have. Lifting the pram up and down the stairs was daily torture and the pub directly below our bedroom would be blasting 'Come on Eileen' until 2am most nights. I remember my sister buying my daughter a dolls' house for Christmas and we didn't have any space to put it, so we had to leave it at my mum's to be played with only occasionally. Shortly after moving back, I made the bold decision that not only was I able to survive being a single mother, but I would set the ambitious goal to purchase a home in a beautiful village close to my family in the countryside. I didn't want my daughter to grow up in central London and I had no hope of giving her a sister, something I desperately wanted to do, in a one-bedroom flat.

Bohemia was due to start school in just over a year and I needed to purchase the home in time to register her for the local village primary. Time would be tight, the money would be a lot, but I knew that there was the possibility I could do it.

Firstly, I got clear on my goal and found out how much I needed. I searched the village online and discovered I could get a small two- to three-bedroom house or bungalow at the bottom end of the market.

Secondly, I took aligned action and sought out a local

mortgage advisor to make sure I wasn't delusional (it's been known) and to find out how much I would need to save.

Thirdly, I prioritised buying this house over *everything* other than looking after my daughter. I fucking hustled.

I started to work shifts that would be illegal if I were working for someone else, starting at 6am and finishing around 11pm, maximising my working time when I was child-free. I would be so tired I would take 15-minute naps on my lash bed between clients.

I ruthlessly decluttered my flat and listed it on Airbnb, renting it out every other weekend then driving me and Bohemia three hours away to stay at my mum's house. Once I saw how much I could make by renting it on Airbnb, I began to rent it out midweek too, on the nights she was with her dad. Where did I sleep? Well, you've guessed it – on my lash bed in the salon! It was quite scary as I felt very exposed with the big salon windows looking out onto the mean streets of north London, but I slid my little treatment room door shut, played a podcast and went to sleep the best I could. I actually never told anybody at the time that I did that. I was too embarrassed. I would get up super early and go shower at my local Soho House (I recognise the irony there) and be back in time for my first client.

I experimented with renting my bedroom too, sleeping in the living area, but after one too many awkward conversations and wondering if I was going to be murdered, I decided I would rather sleep at the salon.

I gave up my home, my personal space, my child-free time and rest for one short year and the result was incredible. I found a little red brick, three-bedroom house with a bay window and a small garden on a cute cul-de-sac opposite a kids' park and I couldn't believe it when I made an offer and it was accepted!

After the year of struggle, I found immense pleasure anytime somebody asked me if I had sold my London flat to move to the country. Everyone who knows me knows I will never sell my London flat and will likely be carried out of there in a box, so I would proudly reply no, this was in fact my second home. That was such a fucking flex! Can you imagine? I was the first out of my friends to get divorced or become a single mother – I moved back to my one-bedroom flat and was working in a relatively low-skilled job and yet here I was, a short year later, with a London flat *and* a little house in the country!

Energetically, I did several things. I visited the village I wanted to move to and took pictures of my daughter wading barefoot through the stream that runs through the centre and put it on my vision board on my phone. I would regularly pass through the village on the way to my mum's house and visit the village shops, acting like a local. Finally, despite saving so hard for that year, I kept my expensive private members' club membership and would often spend sunny mornings around the rooftop pool with Bohemia, eating our breakfast poolside. So many aspects of our lives were compromised, I felt it was really important to not 'feel' poor all the time. I had to remind myself I was a businesswoman hustling to buy a second home, and so that membership reminded me.

By focusing a very short period of my life on one big goal, I was able to achieve in a year what takes others many.

Laser focus 2

Cut to about a year later and I'm eight weeks into my new village and new life when I get two bombshells. Number one is that I'm pregnant with twins. The second is that the world is on the brink of a huge pandemic and about to enter the longest national lockdown in history. In a few short weeks, I had lost both income streams as salons closed and Airbnb travel was cancelled. I found myself isolated with a toddler and a growing bump with mortgages and salon rent to pay (yes, landlords still had to be paid even though we couldn't open!) and a business that was impossible to go back to.

I know some people loved the lockdown, particularly those who locked down in groups and were on furlough, but I sank. I was isolated and alone in some of the hardest possible times in a woman's life: pregnancy, childbirth and the first year. I began to lose my mind. I felt so helpless and so alone, to the point where I questioned if I should abort my babies as I had no means to support myself, and the word on the street was that the hospitals would be full and dying people would be turned away. They literally said that on *This Morning* and I freaked out. We all know what happens in a horror zombie apocalypse movie to the pregnant woman, right?! The idea that I could die giving birth to twins at home alone and leave my daughter motherless was where my head was at.

At my lowest point, I remembered that, up until then, I had been so confident in my ability to manifest my desires and create my own reality. I remembered my power. I decided for no other reason than to give me something to focus on, to begin sharing what I knew with others. This was in the hope that it might help so many who felt hopeless and directionless like me. I learnt how to podcast in an afternoon and purchased a £60 microphone from Amazon which I still use to this day. I posted my first episode and immediately went to number three in the UK charts for self-development. The appetite for people to be able to help themselves with their mindset was clearly there. Within weeks, I had reached the number-one spot, knocking off an established, well-oiled podcast hosted by a celebrity in LA. Love that for me. My bump grew, my babies were born prematurely and, for the first year of their lives, I focused on almost nothing outside of the podcast.

I made money where I could, putting together quite rudimentary manifesting boxes which loyal listeners bought, sending me, pushchair parcel-laden, to the post office every single day. I started a self-development book club which quickly grew to be the largest in the UK and I still run it to this day. As a new mum of twins, I didn't have much time or energy to spare, and so I worked on the podcast with everything I had, to the detriment of a social life, self-care, exercise, dating, travel, adventure – quite frankly, anything.

I truly thank the lockdown now for making my world so impossibly small, and I even thank my postnatal depression as it made me hyper-focus on this one project. And in return, in two short years, this one thing changed my life. It became my business, my purpose, my passion, my calling, but it also gave me money. I needed money. I was able to change so many aspects of my life from that money.

My world had become so small with no travel or adventure. I had no hope of travelling *anywhere* without paying a nanny to come along (it's a whole thing to do with babies under two needing an adult each on a plane) and the money gave me and the girls the opportunity to travel the world like I couldn't have even dreamed of before.

With four of us now in a two-bedroom house, we were cramped and I had no bedroom of my own. That money enabled me to buy my dream home with more than enough bedrooms for all, a dream garden with pool and, best of all, a home office! As you now know, I'm really big on home environment having a huge impact on mothers and I think that's because I spent so many years feeling trapped in mine. Even now, with three young children, it's sometimes easier and preferable to hang out at home than venture out.

Anyway, I hope you can see from these two examples how laser focusing in on one goal, one area, can quickly transform your entire life. And so I ask you this question: what is the one goal you could focus on now that would transform the whole of your life and make your other goals easier?

I hope this chapter has helped you see just how much we as mothers have taken on, much of it unpaid. In order to live your best life, enjoy your family and home, and manifest your goals, time management, prioritisation and creating space in your life are all essential skills to be honed. You have to learn to focus, delegate to others and let some things slide in this overscheduled, cluttered world if you want to manifest like a mother.

What about all that remains? The endless cycles of laundry, cleaning and cooking that have to be done? Guess what, rather than taking away from your manifesting rituals, those tasks can actually *add* to them! Find out how, as we explore turning routines into rituals . . .

Chapter 8

ROUTINES INTO RITUALS

'Now is your chance to infuse your daily motherhood routines with powerful, compounding manifesting rituals.'

What is it you are looking to manifest into your life? Something I know for sure is that your desire will manifest into your reality not because of something you do just once, but rather something you do repeatedly. There are far too many people out there saying you need this £10,000 course, a retreat in Bali where you put coffee up your arse every day for a week or a convention where you walk across burning coals at the end of it, but, truthfully, the real transformation you want to see in your life will come about because of the small changes you make to your every day.

The best way to repeat a positive ritual, technique or practice that is going to help you reach your goals is to make it part of your routine, and if there's one thing us mums live on, its *routine*! Our children thrive on it and our busy lives demand it. Routine is your manifesting bestie.

Now is your chance to infuse your daily motherhood routines with powerful, compounding manifesting rituals. As with everything in this book, its designed to take little to no extra time or energy and has the double benefit of being a positive influence on your children, teaching them how to live well, something that took me almost 15 years of adulthood to figure out.

Mindful Mornings

What does your morning routine look like? An effective morning gratitude and manifesting practice doesn't need to be long or laborious. I know that a written gratitude list is super powerful; however, it always seems overwhelming to me. It feels like the minute I get my pen to paper one of my daughters wakes up and interrupts my ritual, which starts my day off feeling like I've failed already. If your children are older, however, this could totally work for you. Here's what I do instead:

As soon as I wake up, I go into my bathroom and, rather than writing, I *speak* my gratitude and intentions in a ritual I've performed for almost a year now with incredible results.

I recorded a podcast one day with George Lizos who told me one of the most powerful manifesting techniques he used was to send a video or voice note to a friend each and every morning stating exactly how he wanted his day to go and spoke about it in the past tense, as if it had already happened. And so, last summer, I asked my friend Polly if she was willing to try it with me, and she said yes. Each morning now, without fail, I press record and list the things I am thankful for that morning along with my intentions for the day. It's amazing once you start doing this how many days you have lived through without any real direction or intention.

Speaking it out loud to another person forces me to think about what I truly want from my day and how to make it happen. It also highlights to me where I'm being negative, directionless or expecting too much of myself. Sometimes I am able to catch myself and realise that I'm expecting to cram a week's worth of work into one day.

This practice doesn't lead to over-expectation or toxic

positivity; rather, just being mindful about how you want to spend your day. I have days when I declare I'm going to record two amazing podcast episodes or write a chapter of my book or speak at an event with great results. However, other days my intention is simply to slow down, be present with my girls, spend quality time and cook a healthy meal for us as a family. Variety is the spice of life!

Another unexpected benefit of doing this each morning is that as the only adult in my household, it can sometimes get quite late in the day before I speak to another adult, and so it's lovely to be able to start my day off communicating with a good friend. This practice has deepened our friendship immeasurably and given me a valuable insight into how nobody's life is perfect, no matter how it looks on social media.

As I finish my voice note, I turn on my shower and stand at my bathroom window watching the sunrise. Another practice I learnt from Kirsty Gallagher's book *The Goddess Path* was to put my hand over my heart each morning and ask the goddess within myself (bear with me) 'What do you need today?' It's a very simple question that, for me, always gets answered – alternating between:

- rest
- connection
- productivity
- fun
- quality time with the girls
- getting myself/the house straight

It's a great way to ascertain what exactly it is you need to give yourself right now, then plan your day accordingly.

Breakfast Bops

Something I love to do, which makes me sound like I'm in a cult, but I swear it works, is to play a curated playlist of what I call 'gratitude songs' during breakfast. There are some songs out there which are all about the beauty of life, giving thanks, pure gratitude and love. The way I see it, yes it is important to think of things you are thankful for each morning and either write them down or say them out loud, but how much more impactful is it to *sing* it?! By singing it, we are truly feeling it and I often find myself moved to tears during our breakfast routine.

I play the songs through my kitchen smart speaker as I'm preparing breakfasts, packing school lunches and getting ready for the day, and let me tell you, it gets me pumped up!

I have included a selection here that I love for various reasons – check them out and feel free to add your own:

- 'Another Day in Paradise' by Phil Collins: This song is just what you need to remind yourself that if you woke up in a house with food to eat today, you're already winning at life. Sometimes a bit of downward comparison is all you need if you find yourself complaining about all you have.
- 'I Am Blessed' by Eternal: This song reminds you that the love of your family and particularly your children is a priceless gift and is one to be cherished. It is particularly effective if your child has just thrown their breakfast on the floor and you need to be reminded you are blessed.
- 'Thankful' by Beth Hart: This is a beautiful song which expresses the beauty and wonder that is this life.

- 'Gratitude' by Jason Mraz: This is a favourite in my house as not only does it say the words 'thank you' a huge number of times, but it reminds us to be thankful for all the things we take for granted in life, such as the road network, farmers who grow our food and the cleaners who maintain our buildings. It's the ultimate gratitude song!
- 'Vacation' by Dirty Heads: One to listen to if your goal (or reality) is that your job is your calling; if going to work is fun and you would do it for free.
- 'Receive' by Fia: This song is almost religious to me and I play it to remind myself that I am a powerful creator and all I need to do sometimes is allow myself to receive.

Music is both very powerful and incredibly healing. I am a big believer that our words are spells and what you speak out loud, even better if it is sung and repeated with emotion, will manifest into your life.

I've questioned whether to include this section for the sake of my daughters, but I think it's important. When Bohemia was born, she was a much-wanted first baby to me and my husband. I had incredible support as well as a great lifestyle and I fell in love with her immediately. Nobody had warned me about the tidal wave of love that would overcome me and knock me off my feet. When she was three days old, we left the hospital in London where she was born and drove up the A1, stopping halfway at a service station to feed and change her. As we sat down in the service station, a sudden hit of love, stronger than three MDMA pills at once floored me and I just cried and cried with joy. The memory is so beautiful and, eight years later, I can still feel it potently.

When I neared the end of my pregnancy with my twins, I was so excited to feel that rush of love again. My waters broke after a particularly adventurous maternity photoshoot involving a wooden fence and a lace body stocking, and I was rushed into hospital to have an emergency Caesarean section two weeks early. Seeing as they were born during COVID times, just hours after giving birth with fresh surgery wounds and no use of my legs, I was left alone to feed and care for two tiny, premature babies. I was so hyper-focused on caring for this plethora of babies that I didn't feel that instant love. As the days wore on and I finally left hospital, it wasn't to the comfort of my own home as I couldn't drive or lift anything heavy, and so I stayed a couple of days at my mum's house, which was the worst decision ever. It wasn't set up for newborn babies, I was worried about the crying waking my nan at night and hours of painful breastfeeding and mastitis were made even more uncomfortable by being surrounded by people and not in the comfort of my own home. As I was visited by the health visitor, I mentioned that that rush of love hadn't come yet. I wondered more and more anxiously with each passing day if it ever would.

As we returned to the comfort of our own home and settled into our new routine as a family of four, I became increasingly concerned that I didn't love these babies as I should. I googled it for hours on end and couldn't help comparing how I felt to the first time around, but the only advice seemed to be – give it time.

I am fairly certain that what I was going through was post-natal depression as I had some extremely stressful circumstances going on in my life and I was terrified that I would never love them. I cared deeply about their welfare and took excellent care of them, but it was almost like I was a wet nurse for someone else's babies. That feeling is heartbreaking. Have you ever gone on a date with a tall, Canadian doctor who's totally into you and you find yourself willing yourself to like them? It doesn't matter how hard you try, you just can't force that feeling. This was that, times 100. I decided I simply couldn't sit and wait for the feeling to come and so I started to manifest it into my reality, and the number-one way I did that was through the power of music.

As they were being fed, I would put on either Adele's 'Make You Feel My Love' or Dolly Parton's 'I Will Always Love You'. I chose these powerful, emotive songs for their beautiful, love-filled lyrics. As I sang the words to my twins in the early days, it only seemed to heighten the dissonance as I craved that feeling so badly, but slowly, slowly, over time, the words truly became my reality.

I must have done this most days, but the only time I specifically remember is when I had a breakthrough and realised I truly loved them with all my being. We were sitting in my kitchen with them in their little vintage wooden high chairs and I was finally crying tears of joy that I was not only singing the words, but truly, truly feeling them.

As I said, I was a little nervous to share that story as I don't ever want my baby girls to read something that says their mother struggled to love them as newborns, but as a mother of three daughters who will likely go on to experience motherhood struggles of their own, it feels like I'm doing them, and you, my reader, a complete disservice to pretend that this didn't happen. As I look back gently at my experience, I can recognise that I had two completely different birth experiences and that, as a woman in a national lockdown with no business to go back to and no outside physical contact with the world for months on end, it's no wonder I had the experience I did. Had I had more support, more normality in the world, more connection, it probably wouldn't have happened. But it did. I truly believe singing those words with intention every day brought me to the all-encompassing love I feel for them today.

Craft Your Vision

My girls could draw, paint and craft for *hours* and they want nothing more than for me to simply join them and be present. As a busy mum, I used to feel it was such a frustrating waste of my time to sit and draw and paint when I had money to make and so many other responsibilities. That makes me sound like such an ungrateful mother, but we've all been there haven't we? The dinner needs cooking, the bathroom needs cleaning, money needs making and you haven't even had a second to think about your future goals and dreams. This is where a little creativity can make all the difference. I began to sneakily treat the girls' routine crafting time as my manifesting time.

When I lived in London with Bohemia, we would sit and paint or draw most evenings after dinner. As we huddled around the table in my little flat, I would regularly use that time to draw what my next goal was: a proper house in a gorgeous village close to my family. It may not sound like much, but as a newly single mother with only two days a week to work as a beauty therapist, the idea of buying a second home was wild and needed some serious manifesting power! I would take the time to imagine what the windows would look like, the little path leading to the front door or flowers dotting the garden. I would redraw and repaint it with every session until it became my reality. What I love about this is that everyone's a winner. Bohemia was so happy I'd stopped and spent time with her doing something she loves and I had precious time to work on visualising my next goal. Us mums have to be sneaky!

Sweet Dreams to Abundant Reality

No part of the day is more peak 'routine' for families than bed-time. Use this to your advantage by incorporating a simple yet effective bedtime gratitude practice that will not only infuse your bedtime routine with gratitude, but will also bring you closer to your children. However you do bedtime or whatever your sleeping arrangements are, you can make this work for you. For me, we all sleep in a big family bed in my twin daughters' room before they all fall asleep and I creep out to have me time, until, one by one, they follow me into my room. It's like musical beds! As we settle down to sleep, we go around and each say what was the best and the worst thing that happened to us that day. When we started this ritual, my younger daughters Riva and Laveau were very small and didn't really grasp the concept and would state random words like 'unicorn' or 'ice cream' regardless of whether they had encountered them that day or not. Now, through repetition and example, they fully get it.

Examples of their favourite or best things that happened could be a meal we had together, a birthday party they went to, an activity we did or often it's the fact that we are all cosy and snuggling down as a family. Tracing back through their day in their minds encourages them to focus on all the good things that happened to them that day. As we know, what we focus on and give attention to will grow in our lives, so I love to dwell on this part, poring over the numerous small things that happened that day, as they compete to win top spot for that day. Not only that, but through my examples each night they learn to truly feel gratitude for the simple things they may often overlook. The fact that they often say 'my favourite thing is that we're cuddling in bed now' is testament to this practice – that my girls can appreciate this small moment and cherish it; what a result!

For those of you who rigidly stick to the old-school 'positive thoughts only' belief when manifesting or expressing gratitude, there is a very good reason why I include the worst part of our days too. I often ask Bohemia as we walk home from school, 'What happened today?' or 'Any news?' Many mothers will identify when I say I get little to sweet FA in return. It's often after an evening at home decompressing and asking this routine question as we lie in the darkness, sleep getting ever closer, that she will open up. You may find out about a friend they've had a disagreement with, an activity they tried and didn't enjoy or something deeper. I want my daughters to know we can talk openly about everything and that we don't always have to be happy and positive. Discovering the worst parts of your children's days also helps you to plan better days in the future, with their dislikes in mind.

Maybe I'm an attachment parent or maybe I'm an absolute mug, but I *still* lie with all of my daughters until they're asleep, and this used to frustrate me so much! You know what it's like when they're taking forever to go to sleep and it's eating into your precious evening. I now make this time feel better spent by doing two things. The first is that I play subliminal messaging audios while we fall sleep and the second thing is visualisation.

Subliminal messaging

Subliminal messaging works by bypassing the conscious mind and directly influencing the subconscious. Am I saying you can literally manifest and change your life in your sleep? Yes I am!

Subliminal audios contain information that is masked by an overlaid sound or music like rainfall or white noise, so to you, it just sounds like relaxing music. Bedtime is the optimal time to listen as you're in a relaxed or sleep state, which produces theta and delta brainwaves when your mind is more receptive to suggestion. This is because theta waves (just before sleep) are linked to deep learning, intuition and memory formation, and delta waves (deep sleep) allow for cellular healing and subconscious reprogramming.

So, how can subliminals change our behaviour? Scientific studies have shown that even when a message is sped up to the point where it can't be consciously understood and mixed with a music recording, it still has the power to influence our minds. I harness that power by playing soothing subliminals to myself and my daughters every night while we're going in and out of sleep, and I love how easy it makes it to drift off while knowing it's influencing my thoughts for the better, too.

Visualisation

The second piece of the bedtime puzzle for me is visualisation. As I lie there in the darkness, rather than get frustrated or fall asleep only to wake up at 10pm then have insomnia, I create a vivid visualisation in my mind of all that I want to experience, feel and do in the future. I truly believe that visualisation is one of the most powerful manifesting techniques there is and I've dedicated the entire next chapter to it. If you only do one thing to create a better life for yourself, visualise.

Chapter 9

DELIBERATE DAYDREAMING

'Visualisation allows you to mentally rehearse the life you want, helping you align your actions, emotions and mindset with that reality.'

Now that you've embraced the power of turning everyday actions into sacred rituals, let's take the next step in manifesting your dreams.

Sometimes, motherhood can be a scary, boring or isolating time. Even those of us who find great joy in this season of our lives will not be immune to the many challenges the modern mother faces. Something I have discovered is that if your present reality is not what you want to be experiencing, you can begin to create a new reality in your mind and, through regularly visiting this new version of yourself, you begin to take steps towards it.

Visualisation is one of the most powerful tools we mothers can use to shape our reality, both for ourselves and our families. The mind doesn't distinguish between real experiences and vividly imagined ones, meaning that, when you visualise something with clarity and emotion, your brain registers it as if it's already happening. This activates the RAS, which we met in Chapter 1, which starts seeking out opportunities, ideas and people that align with your vision. For busy mothers juggling responsibilities, visualisation can be a grounding practice, whether it's picturing a peaceful home, more financial abundance or better health and energy. It allows you to mentally rehearse the life you want, helping you align your actions, emotions and mindset with that reality.

Scientific studies back up the power of visualisation. Research from Harvard found that people who mentally practised playing the piano for two weeks showed the same brain activity changes as those who physically played it. Another study on Olympic athletes revealed that those who visualised their training saw significant improvements in performance, sometimes even more than those who only physically trained. This is because visualisation strengthens neural pathways, priming the brain and body for success. For mothers, this means that consistently imagining yourself as calm, confident and thriving can help reinforce those qualities in your everyday life. The same applies to manifesting financial goals, attracting supportive relationships or creating a harmonious home environment.

So many highly successful people have credited visualisation as a key tool in their achievements. Did you know that Jim Carrey, before he became a Hollywood superstar, wrote himself a cheque for $10 million for 'acting services rendered'? He carried it in his wallet and visualised himself playing major roles. About six years later, almost exactly as planned, he landed his role in *The Mask*, earning – you guessed it . . . $10 million.

Oprah Winfrey has openly spoken about how she used visualisation to win the role of Sofia in *The Color Purple*. She read the book, fell in love with the story and imagined herself playing the part. When she didn't hear back after auditioning, she kept believing it was meant for her. Shortly after, she got the call from Steven Spielberg offering her the life-changing role.

Have you seen that Arnold Schwarzenegger documentary that was a huge hit on Netflix in 2023? Simply titled *Arnold*? What a masterclass in manifestation! Before becoming a movie star, Arnold Schwarzenegger used visualisation in bodybuilding. He imagined his muscles growing with each workout, picturing himself as Mr Olympia long before he ever won the title. Later, he used the same technique to transition into Hollywood, envisioning himself as a leading man despite his accent and having no acting experience. Wait, didn't he *also* become the governor of California too? The man is a living metamorphosis.

The founder of Spanx, Sara Blakely, who also happens to be the youngest female billionaire (pow!), visualised herself as a successful entrepreneur long before it happened. She credits much of her success to writing down her vision repeatedly, imagining how it would feel to have her own company and be a billionaire.

Will Smith has often talked about the law of attraction and visualisation. He believes that thoughts have physical and measurable power, meaning that the more you focus on an idea, the more real it becomes. He attributes much of his career success to mentally rehearsing his goals and seeing them as already achieved.

Each of these examples showcases how visualisation isn't just about daydreaming; it's a powerful mental practice that aligns thoughts, beliefs and actions towards success. Whether it's in sports, business, acting or any other field, those who master visualisation often turn their dreams into reality.

In my twenties, what I affectionately refer to as my 'ho phase', I had begun dating a footballer and I was absolutely in love with him. It turned out terribly, with him having a secret wife and child, and I was left heartbroken. The whole WAG culture at the time was huge and there were so many dodgy things going on that I felt compelled to write a book about my experiences. So many girls at that time were aspiring to be a WAG and my aim was to warn them it wasn't all fun and games, and to shift their passion and energy on to something better. At the time I was stuck in the same nine-to-five job I'd had for years and the idea of getting a book published was pretty wild – it's not the same as today where you can easily self-publish. I had quite a bit of a commute each day and began to visualise, without knowing it. To begin with, as I mourned the relationship, I would visualise us getting back together somehow, but then, after reading *The Secret*, I began to visualise with intention. I would imagine writing a book all about my experiences, doing book signings, talking about it on TV, making something amazing out of this shitty situation. I would do this every day!

Sure enough, the Universe quickly began to move the people, places and opportunities into my path one by one. I appeared on prime-time TV from which a publisher got in touch and asked me if I could write the entire book in just eight months. From there, I contacted the BBC who were making a documentary on the WAG culture that was sweeping the nation and they asked me to be a part of the show, covering the whole writing and publication process. During those long days in a job I hated with a daily commute, I had unwittingly created an incredibly powerful visualisation practice which had quickly manifested my desire. I was no longer the sad-sack girl who had been dumped and simply returned to her boring nine-to-five life; I had created an incredible opportunity out of it and the proceeds of that book allowed me to purchase my first ever property – that little flat above the pub in north London which I adored.

The great news is that boring desk job and long commute were examples of low cognitive tasks where I was required to be physically doing something, but it didn't take much mental capacity. As we saw in the last chapter, motherhood is packed with these kinds of activities during which we are able to consciously visualise. Long feeding sessions, afternoon walks with the pram, the school run, folding laundry . . . these are all times during which you are free to visualise. So, instead of pulling out your phone to mindlessly scroll yet again, create a vivid visualisation.

My Guide to Effective Visualisation

So, what makes an effective visualisation? Firstly, it must be compelling. It must excite you! The best visualisations tend to come naturally as almost fantasising – imagining yourself as your best self, living your best life. Is it you on your future wedding day looking and feeling great, marrying the love of your life? Is it your child who has been plagued with colic sleeping through the night effortlessly and you waking up rested and happy? Is it you being a boss bitch, making loads of money and buying an incredible car? Is it your school-refusing child finding the courage and support to return to school, happily waving to you as they go in?

Whatever your vision, give it as much energy as you can. Remember the old saying: where attention goes, energy flows. Make your vision bold and bright, visualise to music if that helps and give your vision aspects from all your senses: for example, how do you feel, what do you smell, what can you taste?

A few years ago, I wanted this very specific feeling of being on a boat, day drunk on rosé, the sun on my skin, sea salt in the air, having the time of my life. This visualisation was initially a 'happy place' to go to during a meditation, but the more I did it, the more I realised I wanted this experience IRL. It was fun to visualise something purely for pleasure – not some huge goal! No more than six months later, my American friends, who I meet up with each year, invited me to Cabo San Lucas in Mexico.

Our trips were usually to cities, not resorts and we would spend time exploring and drinking, so imagine my surprise when they said we would be staying at a beachside resort and on one day we would be taking a boat out on the ocean! Yes – I was ready. That day, we had a fabulous time, drinking rosé in the sun and swimming with the most colourful fish you can imagine. As I lay out on the front of the boat, with the sun on my skin and the sea salt in the air, I realised that this was exactly what I had been replaying in my mind.

That actually reminds me of another powerful visualisation that happened that very day. I had a habit for a while of buying myself gold Cartier bracelets every time I hit a new financial goal. I swiftly stopped after a visit to Pitsea Market in Essex only to discover everyone and their hairdresser had a fake one. Anyway, that's beside the point. I had a beautiful gold bangle engraved on the inside with a money goal I had reached. It was very symbolic, not to mention expensive AF. As I jumped off the boat, my bangle must have been unscrewing slowly and it came off. I looked at my arm – it was gone. Cue me acting like Kim Kardashian when she lost her diamond earring in the ocean.

A few guys from the boat donned snorkels and attempted to find it, but after about 30 minutes, I truly had made peace with not getting it back. I simply wasn't attached to the outcome. As they gave up one by one, the captain of the boat was like, 'No, I will try one last time.' Just to give you an image here, we are out in the middle of the ocean, the sea bed is about ten metres below – ten metres! I said, 'Hold on, before you do, I'm just going to visualise.' I closed my eyes and imagined the captain rising to the surface, bangle in hand. I visualised us all cheering and me thanking him. I visualised myself telling this story on my podcast the following week. About three or four minutes after this visualisation, the captain comes up to the surface with not one, but both separate pieces of the bangle held above his head!

The lesson here?

- If you're trying to find something: visualise an amazing outcome.
- If you're taking a test: visualise an amazing outcome.
- If you want to succeed at something: visualise an amazing outcome.

It works in every circumstance.

Visualisation is more than just a practice; it's a portal to the life you're calling in. Every time you show up for yourself in this way, you're shifting timelines, reprogramming your subconscious and opening the doors to a reality beyond your wildest dreams. Are you ready? Let's begin.

Step one: See it as already done

Find a quiet space, close your eyes and let yourself drift into the version of you who already has it all. See the details, the colours, the textures, the people, the moments. If you're manifesting love, picture yourself waking up next to your soulmate, feeling their warmth beside you. If it's success, imagine the email, the call, the yes you've been waiting for. Make it feel real. Because, in a way, it already is.

Step two: Speak it into reality

Words hold power. Speak your desire as if it's already happening. Start with, 'I am so happy and grateful now that . . .' and let the words flow. For example, 'I am so happy and grateful now that I am in the most loving, aligned relationship of my life', 'I am so happy and grateful now that money flows to me effort-lessly and abundantly' or 'I am so happy and grateful now that I wake up every morning in my dream home, filled with light and love.' You could also write this down in your journal.

Step three: Feel it in your bones

The Universe doesn't respond to words alone, it also responds to your energy. So, let yourself feel it. Breathe in the joy, the excite-ment, the deep gratitude. Imagine your whole body filling up with the energy of your desire. The more you feel it, the faster it arrives.

Step four: Make it a daily ceremony

The magic happens in the repetition. At whatever point in your day feels spacious for you to be able to do so, return to your vision. Even if it's just for two minutes, remind yourself that it's already yours.

Step five: Follow the breadcrumbs

Your manifestations don't just show up out of the blue, you co-create them. Pay attention to the nudges, the little pulls, the feeling in your gut guiding you towards action. Maybe it's send-ing a message, applying for something or showing up in a new way. Trust that the path is unfolding perfectly, step by step.

Remember, this is your story, your movie, your dream unfold-ing in real time. Show up for it. Trust it. The Universe is already rearranging itself to meet you where you are. You are so much closer than you think.

What I love about visualisation is that, one day, you will be in the middle of your real life and you will suddenly become aware that you are indeed in the exact situation you used to play on repeat in your mind. As Bob Proctor once said: 'If you can see it in your mind, you'll hold it in your hand.'

Now that you've visualised your dream life, we are going to dive into such a lovely practice, and one that as a single mother I adore doing for myself. Let's explore the beautiful act of taking care of your future self.

Chapter 10
FUTURE YOU

'Taking care of your future self is really important because it is a physical action you take to make life cushty for future you – because you love that bitch!'

I used to really struggle with low attendance – it was a dirty streak that followed me my entire life; from my very first day at school, all through college and even at work. I'd find it a real effort to get up and get motivated, and so would hardly ever show up. I was unreliable, work-shy and never on time. What a shit show! When I first read *The Secret* and discovered that I could change any aspect of my life with the law of attraction, it was blindingly obvious which area of my life was causing me so much pain.

I didn't want to go to my office job anymore. I hated authority, I hated the commute, I hated rush hour, I hated dressing for the office, I hated the air con, I hated the corporate vibes. I hated it all! The ultimate goal was to be able to work for myself. What exactly I would do working for myself didn't even really matter – it was just the freedom I craved; the freedom to wear what I want, to get up when I want, to spend a warm day out in the sun, not shivering in an air-conditioned office with a load of old men.

I had a side hustle as a spray-tanner at the time which I did in my tiny kitchen in the evenings and weekends around my full-time job. I loved it, I was good at it and it was easy

money! The problem was my life experience had built a massive limiting belief in my mind – I didn't believe I could ever
show up for myself and my business because my entire track
record was that I was unreliable, late and work-shy. My entire
life – from my first day at school up until that present day in my
mid-twenties – said so. If I quit my job to become a spray-tanner
full time, I believed I would let down clients, lie in bed all day,
be late and do a shit job – because that had been my work
life MO! I had proven to myself over and over again that was
who I was. But then something incredible happened. When I
did eventually make that leap (massively encouraged by an
ex, thank goodness!), I valued my new way of life so much
that I was never going to go back to working for someone else
ever again. I started to show up for myself in lots of small ways.
I would respond to messages quickly, book clients in and show
up every single time. I was on time, did a good job and saw my
business grow as a result. Over time, I began to trust myself more
and more, because of the way I had been showing up in the
business. I trusted myself enough to hire an assistant, I trusted
myself enough to rent a room in a salon and eventually to buy
my own salon and have multiple people working for me. In a
few short years I went from the girl who would rarely turn up to
work to becoming the boss myself, buying a premises, tanning
celebrities live on TV and having people work for me. What a
fucking turnaround!

So what changed? Why did my life suddenly get so much
better? I had slowly, slowly, one day at a time and one client
at a time, built an unshakeable trust with myself. I now trusted
myself completely if I had bigger aspirations, because I knew
with certainty that I was the kind of person who would show up,
do the best job and keep it moving. Not only that, but I began
to build an incredible self-love too. That love hadn't always

been there. How could I love the girl who let her twenties slip away, one year after another, cooped up in some shitty office block, suffocating her dreams? But this bitch? This bitch who had the courage to leave that job, that security and pursue her dreams and work for herself? I damn *loved* her. She showed up every day and did the best job possible so I got to live this life of freedom that I loved so much.

A way to build this unshakeable self-love and self-trust in your life is to take action for your future self.

Think of the Future to Take Action in the Present

While it's important to be present in the moment, looking out for your future self really is the ultimate act of mindfulness because you are no longer putting off changes that will impact you going forward. You are turning that 'someday' into today.

Taking action for your future self is one of the most powerful ways to create personal growth and lasting success. It's a true act of self-care – one that strengthens both self-love and self-trust. When it comes to manifesting the things we desire, whether it's a dream career, love, financial abundance or even a baby, our ability to attract them is directly linked to how worthy we believe we are. The more we show up for ourselves today, the more we expand our sense of worthiness, allowing us to receive all that we truly desire.

Taking care of your future self is really important because it is a physical action you take to make life cushty for future you – because you love that bitch! If you didn't love yourself, you wouldn't want to make decisions that benefit future you. When you consistently make these changes, you build this incredible self-love, trust and respect.

Taking action for your future self doesn't have to mean making big moves; sometimes it's the smallest of changes that build to make a big difference. This is an idea I came across after seeing one of my listeners on Instagram take care of her future self after a night out. I was fascinated. As she went out to a Christmas party, she had folded back the duvet on her bed, left two bottles of water on the nightstand along with painkillers, a set of pyjamas and an eye mask. For years and years, I had rolled in after nights out only to fall onto my bed, still dressed, cold and uncomfortable. I would lie in the darkness for hours, slowly turning to dust and dreaming of the glass of water that would make my hangover the next day so much better. I literally couldn't believe that someone had taken the time to ensure that future them was taken care of! This was such a wild idea to me. On my next night out (and I get terrible hangovers by the way – I'm pretty sure I'm intolerant to alcohol as both my mum and sister don't drink because of the terrible after-effects), I decided to put this into practice.

Instead of getting ready and running out of the door leaving my room in a mess, I cleared away the clothes and make-up, folded back my blanket so I could simply fall into bed, left a big bottle of apple juice next to my bed (I crave apple juice during a hangover – who knows why) as well as some painkillers and make-up wipes on my pillow. What a bloody game changer! You better believe, when I got home that night I felt so taken care of. I cleaned my face, drank the juice, popped the pills and felt so much better for it in the morning. I think that's the aspect of it that I love the most – the fact that I did feel so taken care of, even if it was by a past version of me! As someone who has been single for almost six years at the time of writing, I crave that feeling of being looked after.

As a single mother, nobody really takes care of me and, it

doesn't matter how old we are, we all want to be taken care of – right? I imagine that some of you will have amazing partners who make you feel taken care of, but, for me and so many other mothers (whether they are single or not), it's simply not our reality. By our very nature, mothers are caregivers and if we have to get nurtured by our goddamn past selves, so be it!

When manifesting a life you want with all of your goals coming to fruition, you are only able to manifest what you truly believe you deserve and what you are able to receive. If you are going through life surviving one day at a time and not being the beneficiary of any little luxuries, you will be unable to receive luxury and care in your life. This is the hard truth – sometimes the only person who is going to take care of you and make your life beautiful is *you*.

I walked through life for years expecting so little for myself and my day-to-day experiences. The hangover example is just one of many. After that, I was off. I began to plan and set up life to make it as easy and pleasant as possible for this current version of me who was undoubtedly in the hardest era of motherhood in her goddamn life. I now infuse love and care for my future self all over my life:

- As I mentioned in Chapter 6, I now always keep my car stocked with essentials – snacks, water bottles, baby wipes, a blanket and a phone charger. It means that no matter what the day throws at me, I'm prepared. Whether it's an unexpected traffic jam, a hungry toddler meltdown or realising my phone is on 2 per cent battery, I know my future self will be grateful I took the time to do this.
- Each night, I lay out clothes for myself and the girls. Mornings are chaotic enough without having to make

decisions before I'm fully awake. Having everything ready means I can start the day feeling calm instead of frantically digging through drawers or dealing with last-minute outfit battles. Morning version of me deserves that.

- I prep breakfasts and lunches ahead of time so that the mornings run smoother. Even something as simple as soaking oats overnight or packing the kids' school lunches before bed makes all the difference. It's a small act of care for my future self, ensuring she doesn't have to rush around in the morning when time always seems to disappear.

- Every night, I do a quick ten-minute reset – tidying the kitchen, fluffing the sofa cushions and putting toys back in their baskets – so I can wake up to a home that feels fresh and peaceful. There's nothing worse than starting the day feeling like I'm already behind, so I do this little act of kindness for myself, knowing it will make tomorrow easier.

As you can see, there are a million little things you can do to care for your future self, but this technique also applies to bigger events.

A couple of years ago, I read an incredible book called *Calm Christmas and a Happy New Year* by Beth Kempton and it absolutely transformed how I viewed the festive season. I am hyper-aware of how many magical Christmases I get to enjoy with my children while they are young and have made it my mission to make every single one count. In the past, I had started shopping way too late, was breaking my back wrapping on the floor at midnight on Christmas Eve and would rush out the door looking and feeling harassed for my annual mums'

Christmas night out. Beth's wise words taught me that a little forward planning and energy management meant I could create a Christmas season with my daughters that felt as good in real life as it looked on Instagram.

I began by doing all of my shopping and wrapping in November, giving myself ample time to choose presents wisely, find hidden treasures and not panic buy/overspend. Getting that huge part of Christmas stress out of the way in relatively boring November left the whole of December free for me to be present and enjoy the season.

Buying and wrapping is probably a mother's biggest job at Christmas and so I decided to make it a fun experience for myself. I saved up episodes of my favourite murder podcast or listened to Beth's *The Calm Christmas* podcast (slightly cheerier) as I wrapped and dedicated our guest room as a 'present room' with everything I needed to wrap to hand. I bought festive snacks and my favourite drink and made a few fun evenings of it. My evenings up there wrapping to my favourite podcasts are now a sacred part of my festive traditions.

I also started scheduling in my Christmas nights out in about September, before all the good dates were taken. I remember reading once that when you see people who are living a fun and full life – out at a BBQ, off to the races with friends, on the beach in Cornwall – none of that is accidental. Those people have planned and organised and made those events happen. It sounds obvious, but it's true! I used to always feel so jealous of people who managed to get away to Cornwall each summer, living it up on the gorgeous beaches (accommodation gets booked up notoriously early!) and, after reading this, I realised I just needed to plan fun things in advance. And so now in February I book my summer trip to Cornwall and on 1 September I message all my friends and get the best Christmas dates booked in. As a mum I am *tired* and to fully enjoy a festive night out I have to have the time and space beforehand to get ready, feel my best and also have just rested so I can have fun! Scheduling my nights out when the girls are with their dads so I can get ready in peace and luxuriate in my hangover is honestly such energy management.

I said no to overscheduling the festive season, to a million Santa visits (one is enough) and all the overcrowded events that overstimulate my children and always seem to be a let-down, and instead focused on the things that bring us joy and we never seem to find the time to do. For us, that was making Christmas cookies with my mum, snuggling up to watch Christmas movies, making paper chains and Christmas cards, having games nights and hosting our now annual gingerbread party.

Deferring (is it still called deferring if you do it earlier?!) all the hard work to November really created space for me to be a rested, fun, happy version of me with the time and energy to wash my hair and put on a bit of make-up. What a time to be alive.

As I've mentioned, every New Year's Eve I host a goal-setting party for the year ahead. Part of my method that works so well is setting goals for each quarter of the year, and often the point of my first quarter/winter goals are so that future me can thrive! On the second winter of living in my new house, I took action in the dead of winter to transform the front of my property. I have quite a big front garden and driveway, but it was totally unusable as cars tend to speed down my country lane and I was terrified of the girls running out onto the road. In addition, the entire driveway was rough gravel so the girls couldn't walk barefoot or play on it. Winter me set about getting strong, tall gates put on the front to protect the girls and our home, and the driveway was transformed into a smooth, resin racetrack. On that very first day of spring when the sun reappeared after a long winter, the girls closed the gates, got out their scooters and spent the entire day out there. With my front door wide open and the sound of the girls all laughing and playing outside, I really thanked winter me for getting that done. It has improved the quality of our home life so much.

When you do something for your future self with intention, you double the power of it. Not only are you saying, 'I'm a worthy bitch and I deserve a good future', you are also saying, 'I'm a magical bitch and I am doing this now because your future is going to be wild!'

One example of this is, about a year into hosting my podcast, I realised the importance of posting stories and showing my face. I realised with horror that my teeth were really quite wonky! As an intentional move, saying to the Universe, 'I am going to become known for my podcast, my face will be out there and I will look the part', I booked in to get Invisalign orthodontic treatment to straighten my teeth. It was very unpleasant for about a year and a half, but it was so worth it! I now find myself in so many situations where I would have felt really self-conscious otherwise – walking the red carpet at the BAFTAs, photoshoots, influencer events that are being filmed and hosting my own live shows to over 800 people. I truly believe that intentional action for future me literally propelled me to the future I desired.

Treat Yourself How You Want Others to Treat You

What I've noticed about treating myself better is that it teaches other people and the Universe how to treat me too. It sets a standard. Since being a single mother, I've not bothered much with days like my birthday or Mother's Day. I'm at an age and living in a time where we have single-tap checkouts on all of our favourite online stores and a definite 'treat yo'self' culture. As a result, my family and friends don't really get me anything. I know some women have amazing co-parents who celebrate them on their birthday or Mother's Day, but that ain't my reality! My daughters' birthdays would be celebrated with cakes, presents, balloons, a party, but my own not so much. About three years ago, all that changed. Through a combination of inner child work, divine feminine energy work and also a dose of money mindset, I started to make a habit of purchasing myself a really boujee gift and celebrating my birthday and Mother's Day. What's fun is that these gifts were better than anything I had received from any dusty old man in the past. The presents would arrive, elaborately gift wrapped from Selfridges or NET-A-PORTER with a gift note: 'To Me, From Me. You deserve it, I love you, thank you for making our life amazing.' It felt really special!

Then something amazing happened. My daughters saw my worth, followed my lead and began to treat my birthday and Mother's Day like the big events they are! This year, for the first time, my daughter Laveau started drawing endless pictures of me, complete with big lashes, a crown and eternally pregnant with *just* her, not her twin sister, and put them all into a book to gift me. Every single day for about a month before she would squirrel these pictures away in a box and get her sister Riva to draw some too to surprise me on the big day! About two weeks before, she told me I needed to order a cake for my birthday from the man who makes all their celebration cakes. It hadn't occurred to me to order a cake for myself and so I got a gorgeous pink vintage-style heart. Finally, on my birthday morning, I was told to stay in bed and all three of them scurried off downstairs, plotting and planning. When I *was* allowed in my own kitchen, what I saw brought tears to my eyes. With cushions, blankets and a low table, they had fashioned together what I can only describe as a hospital bed, appropriately right next to the wine fridge, and had laid out a breakfast of melon, along with forks for all of us. They had each made a card and playing in the background was relaxing spa music. It was genuinely the most thoughtful, special morning and I will remember it forever.

You don't always get the loving partner who picks the perfect gift, you don't always get the thoughtful ex who helps your child to get you a card, sometimes you don't even have the family or friends who stop to make your day special – what I've realised in this life is that sometimes you have to raise the standards for yourself first then everyone else will meet you there. It takes time, energy and conscious effort to raise the bar of what you think you deserve, but it's vital manifesting work as it is paralleled by what the Universe can deliver for you. I come from a line of mothers who never ever took time away from their children to celebrate themselves and that's something I've had to unlearn. Here I am, fresh from my 40th birthday where I spent the *entire* month celebrating – a weekend away with my mum friends, a family trip to Dubai and, finally, five days child-free with my best friends in the Bahamas! I was determined that my 40th would be one to remember. Because I'm worthy. Because my children deserve to have a mother who is happy and fulfilled. Because I can. Because the more I value myself, the more I'm able to manifest.

How you treat your future self is such a vital part of living your best life, because it's the ultimate act of mindfulness. I like to think of myself as a little butler to future me, making her life so nice, so easy and so fulfilling – because I love and cherish that bitch! So whether it's doing garden work in winter so you can enjoy the summer, wrapping all your gifts in November so you can celebrate the festive season in December or having dental work in 2022 so you can have straight teeth in 2023 – do something today your future self will thank you for!

Let's take a step back from the future and focus on right now. One of the most transformative and quite frankly magical acts of mindfulness is the art of romanticising your life, as well as fully *embodying* the woman you want to become, through your daily habits, the way that you dress and even the theme tune you have playing in your head as you walk down the street – and you're going to love it!

Chapter 11

THE WOMAN YOU WANT TO BECOME

**'Our aim is to wake up every day and live
our lives as though we already have
our goal manifested. We already have it.
We *are* that bitch.'**

I am so excited to share this chapter with you! There are so
many fun concepts and techniques here to not only get
you living your best life right now, but also manifesting the
life of your goddamn dreams in real, actionable, tangible
ways – not just sitting and meditating to the moon with your
tits out.

A big part of manifesting what you desire is simply being
on the vibration of what you want to attract. It's so simple,
yet when you try to feel and embody being happy, rich, successful, loved, fit, fulfilled – whatever it is for you – through
traditional manifesting techniques alone (such as journaling,
meditation, and so on) it's a *slog*.

Our aim is to wake up every day and live our lives as
though we already have our goal manifested. We already
have it. We *are* that bitch. There are three powerful concepts that I've discovered over the years which I feel have
helped me achieve what I want not only faster, but also
while having fun:

- The art of romanticising your life.
- Stepping into main character energy.
- Dressing for the life you want.

Let's look at each of those now.

The Art of Romanticising Your Life

Have you heard about this trend? I must admit I was a little late to it, being a TikTok philistine. However, once I did discover it, there was no stopping me. My self-development book club and I spent an entire month delving into this topic and I bloody loved it! Romanticising your life combines gratitude, mindfulness, positive psychology and *hygge*. It is about seeing the magic in the everyday and shifting your perspective so that even the most mundane, routine moments feel special. It's not about grand gestures or living in a fantasy – it's about finding beauty in the small things, being present and treating your daily life as something to be cherished rather than just another list of tasks to get through. It's about being thankful for what life is offering you right now; you can't always control what is happening in your life, after all. But you *can* choose how you respond to and enjoy it. Romanticising your life is like living your gratitude journal out loud.

It's easy to feel like life is amazing on those rare days I get to go to a swanky event or lie on a beach, but the reality is the majority of my time is spent mothering tiny humans, and that can be fucking grim at times. Learning this hack has transformed that for me!

As mothers, we can get so caught up in survival mode that we forget to appreciate the little joys that are already woven into our days. Romanticising your life is about lighting a candle while you do the evening tidy-up, playing music while making breakfast or sipping your coffee slowly instead of gulping it down on the go. It's about making space for simple pleasures, turning the ordinary into something that feels extraordinary – and it only takes a little conscious effort.

When it comes to manifesting, the energy we live in daily is what we attract more of. If we're constantly in a state of stress, exhaustion and overwhelm, we're telling the Universe that's our norm. But when we start to infuse our days with small rituals of beauty, pleasure and mindfulness, we shift into an energy of abundance, joy and self-worth, making it easier to attract what we truly desire. For mothers, this means taking small steps to elevate our surroundings and experiences, which we already talked a little bit about in Chapter 6. This might be setting intentions for the day and greeting the morning while sipping tea, dressing in a way that makes you feel confident or packing a 'mum bag' for your next soft play visit containing your favourite book and a snack you love. When we treat ourselves with care, we tell the Universe we are worthy of more.

Applying this to your manifesting journey as a mother means recognising that your current reality isn't something to escape from, it's something to elevate. Instead of waiting for the dream home, the dream job or the dream relationship to feel happy and fulfilled, you start bringing that feeling into your life now. You create a home that feels like a sanctuary, even if it's filled with toys and laundry piles. You make space for self-care, even if it's just five minutes of deep breathing before the school run. The more you lean into this, the more your reality shifts, because the version of you who has everything she desires isn't just in the future – she's already here, waiting for you to embody her now.

I remember Samantha Hearne, while a guest on my podcast, saying that so many mothers give excuses of why they can't do what they want to do, why they can't work on themselves or their own lives: 'I have a newborn', 'I have a toddler', 'I have a school-refusing child', and so on . . . The fact is, that's not an excuse why you can't, it's simply your reality. The ones who succeed are the ones who look around at their reality, improvise, adapt and overcome, as the US Amry Marines would say. Will you keep loyal to your excuses? Or will you improvise, adapt and overcome?

There's a great movie called *Isn't It Romantic* which I would love you to watch as you experiment with romanticising your own life. It's a great romcom that perfectly captures the magic of romanticising life. The film follows Natalie, a cynical architect who suddenly finds herself trapped in a cliché romcom world after an accident. What makes this movie stand out is how it makes you lol but also gives you a deeper message about how we often overlook the beauty of our own lives. If you're into romanticising your life, this film encourages you to see life through a lens of possibility, magic and joy. It shows how we can turn even the most mundane moments into something special by shifting our mindset. The goal with romanticising your life is to create pockets of magic throughout your day when you can. I cannot describe to you how amazing it feels when you've mastered this, but it's incredible!

One Christmas, I had a weekend booked in London to record a podcast and have some nights out with my friends, and I had just discovered the power duo: romanticising your life and main character energy (more on this in a bit!). Rather than just seeing this as a normal, winter weekend in London, I decided to make the conscious decision to imagine my life as a Richard Curtis romcom. At this point, I had been single and probably celibate if we're honest for a good few years at least. I packed my weekend bag full of outfits that made me feel my best (also more on *this* later!) and took the time to tan and get a blow-dry. As I set foot out of my little London apartment door, I was open to all kinds of fun and random romcom-style shit to happen to me! I could literally hear a theme tune playing as I walked. The gorgeous glow of a festive pre-Christmas London all lit up only helped.

That afternoon, I met my two friends for lunch and we decided to go to a popular restaurant behind Selfridges. As we walked to the front reception, I locked eyes *as if I were in a romcom* with the most beautiful man I have ever seen (he turned out to be the restaurant manager). The space between making eye contact and getting our words out seemed to go on forever. My friends and I took a table and, as we caught up and had some wine, I noticed the manager's eyes and mine kept meeting across the room. Even my friends noticed it. Towards the end of our time there, I went to the bathroom and, when I came back, one of my friends had boldly made a move and got his number for me. Shout out to Julee, doing the Lord's work. We had a chat and I promised to call him later, once I was home. As we parted ways and I headed to east London to meet my other friend, Polly, I was virtually skipping down the street. As someone in their late thirties, I often noticed that even on nights out or adult-only holidays, there were very few men in the wild I found attractive and, even if I did, we're at an age now where most people are married or whatever and connections are *rare*. And so, it seemed absolutely wild to me that simply by romanticising my life and approaching the day expecting fun, random, romantic things to happen to me, they magnetised into my reality! (In case you are at all invested in this man and this story, we were messaging all evening and let's just say he popped over for a nightcap later that night. He had the most captivating eyes I've ever seen, but it wasn't love. What it was, however, was a very fun encounter that transformed a normal Saturday into my very own romcom.)

How to make the ordinary seem special

Romancing the ordinary makes so much sense, because the ordinary is what makes up the majority of our lives. At the end of every calendar year, I'm one of those annoying people who makes a reel of my highlights from that year (let me live my life – it brings me so much joy!). But as I think about the reality of those highlight reels, they only include the anomalies in my year: the far-flung holidays, the big events, the nights out, the red carpets, the launch of this book probably. But those events make up so little of my actual real life – each one just a few hours or a couple of days at the most in the whole year. These are the stars amidst the darkness (the darkness being the vast majority of life). Those daily, mundane tasks that can all merge together – that's what we spend the majority of our lives doing. A lot of our lives are on repeat, especially for mothers, as our children thrive on the routines we build.

This is your PSA to not wait until that holiday or birthday to really live life, but to enjoy every day where you can. This trend emerged in the depths of the pandemic as people struggled with their worlds becoming so small and so slow. It encourages you to raise your vibration and start showing up for the smallest moments in your daily life. How can you elevate your morning shower, your commute to work, the weekly baby group or your bedtime routine? How can you infuse the ordinary with magic? How can you make even the most mundane of days feel unique and special? Let me give you some examples . . .

The endless newborn feeding and changing cycle:

It's cute when everyone comes to visit, but when you're weeks or months in and life feels like it's been an endless, thankless cycle of feeding and changing, instead of feeling hopeless and like you're never going to get your life back, why not embrace this season? Could you slow down with it? During these first months, your baby needs you (and your tits if you're breastfeeding!) to be physically close at all times. That's just your reality for now. Transform the way you see those four walls closing in on you by creating a little nest and making it as cosy as possible – Netflix at hand, a pile of books you've been meaning to read by your side. Relish in your favourite podcasts, shows and books, knowing that real life will reappear soon enough.

Breakfast: I'm such a basic bitch when it comes to breakfast, either skipping it entirely or grabbing something on the go. Recently, my daughters and I went to Dubai and so enjoyed the change in our daily breakfast routine, sitting down together to really savour it. I had avocado and eggs which I looked forward to all the other 23 hours of the day I wasn't eating it and Riva discovered a love of Greek yoghurt and honey. Not every morning, but on weekends now, I recreate that vacay breakfast with fruits, eggs, toast, avocado and yoghurts all laid out for us to enjoy together.

Your evening meal: Family mealtimes are rapidly vanishing as a thing of the past and so it is our duty to preserve them! When I was younger, we would all eat around the dinner table, never on the sofa, in front of the TV or on our laps. Today, I make sure we still sit around the table together. I dim the lights, light a candle for the table and give out jobs to the girls, such as putting out cutlery or making drinks. As the only adult, it can be tempting to just feed them all quickly and then relax and eat on my own later (and I definitely went through phases of this), but, as a mother, it's my job to not only teach but demonstrate to my daughters how to live well. And a part of living well is enjoying the nightly ritual of a family meal together, sharing food, telling stories and just being. If I wait until my toddlers will sit properly at the table or until we all want to eat the same thing, I will be waiting forever. Remember: improvise, adapt, overcome.

Your evening bath: Is this just an opportunity to get clean or could you take the extra time to light a candle or two, pour in some detoxifying ingredients (Bentonite clay and Epsom salts; you're welcome), put on a meditation or your favourite podcast and line up your go-to skincare products to give yourself a little facial?

Soft play – the bane of my life: Rather than just packing for the girls then sitting there bored and drinking an overpriced hot chocolate, I now pack for myself too! I ask myself, what could elevate my experience today? And so I pack myself a flask of my favourite drink, some snacks and the book I'm reading. I actively try to not be the mum at soft play looking at my phone rather than at my children, but, for the love of God, I've watched you come down that slide for two years now! Instead, I model reading for fun to my children. Try it – the difference is amazing! You will still be interrupted from your reading 500 times, but you don't feel like a terrible mother in an episode of *Black Mirror* giving more of your life energy to your phone than your child.

Elevate your spaces: Whatever spaces you spend your time in, how can you make them the most practical, comfortable and enjoyable they can be? My home office is a small room right at the top of my house in the eaves. Up here is just a guest room, bathroom and the office. The small windows overlook a country lane and the farmer's fields with the city in the distance. Today, as I write this, it's a cold, dark winter's afternoon and it could potentially be a bit creepy and isolating being up here all by myself with the rest of the house in darkness. Instead, I decided to visualise this little office as my cosy work nest, lit up and warm while the wind and rain lashes outside. I have a little radiator plugged in under my desk, a warm lamp glows in the corner and a squashy pink chair by my bookcase offers a comfortable place to read or take a break when my back has had enough of being at my desk. This formula can be applied to a number of different spaces or scenarios – whether it's your kitchen as you're making dinner or your bedroom as you're putting away the laundry. Make it a vibe!

Romanticising your life not only transforms your ordinary moments and makes you feel more alive, it helps you smash your daily gratitude quota. Rather than simply thinking about what you're grateful for or writing a list, why not take that moment while you're living it and infuse whatever it is you're doing with gratitude and intention?

Another benefit to romanticising your life is that it gives a feeling of control where often there's none. Let me explain: imagine you have a horrid commute to work; it's cold and raining and the traffic is always terrible. Rather than rushing, driving off with your coat on and huffing the whole way at how long it's taking, perhaps you clear out your car, heat it up so you can take your coat off and feel comfortable, line up your favourite podcast to listen to and prepare a healthy grazing bowl and juice to enjoy on the way. By the time you arrive at work, you're ready for the day ahead from having created this little space for yourself to relax and enjoy the journey.

You will just *know* when you have successfully captured the essence of romanticising your life – you'll feel it. It's like receiving a text from somebody you've been waiting to hear from or that first ray of spring sunshine hitting your skin after a long, dark winter. It's *delicious*. What naturally follows on from this is main character energy.

Stepping Into Main Character Energy

Have you ever met somebody who just seems like the main character of their own story? Maybe they have an aspirational morning routine, spend time taking care of themselves and genuinely enjoy their life. We can always spot these people and wish we could be like them, but, spoiler alert: we can be them at any time! We just have to start.

I always find it so interesting when a group of independent adults gets together for a holiday – hen parties are especially great for this. Everyone is in the same environment and yet people all have their own routines, rituals and ways of doing things. Maybe I'm a secret anthropologist, but colour me intrigued. It's always so fascinating to me how people choose to start their day, what they eat and the environment they set up around themselves. Will they get up at dawn and go for a run before breakfast or will they still be out from the night before?

When I went to Cabo a couple of years ago with my friends from the US, maybe it was the jet lag, but I was up with the sunrise each morning and chose to go outside and write my gratitude list overlooking the ocean before anyone was awake. That felt so good for my day and for my life to do that.

I am somebody who loves to have a muse. I love to see examples of people living the kind of life I want, because it shows me it's possible! Having a muse or a role model is like having a guiding light – a version of who you want to become reflected back at you through someone else's energy, confidence and choices. It's not at all about copying another person's life, but about seeing what's possible and allowing it to expand your own vision. As mothers, it's easy to lose ourselves in the daily demands of caring for others, but having a muse helps us reconnect with our own desires, style and ambitions. It could be a woman you admire for her grace and strength, a celebrity who embodies confidence, a mother whose parenting style you love or even a fictional character who moves through life with fun and adventures along the way. When we start asking ourselves, 'What would she do? How would she show up today?', we step into a version of ourselves that feels more empowered, inspired and in control of our own narrative.

This is where main character energy comes in. Instead of feeling like a supporting act in everyone else's story, a role model reminds you to romanticise your own life, take up space and move through your days with a sense of purpose. She inspires you to put on the outfit that makes you feel amazing, to take that small daily action towards your dream or to say no to things that don't align with your highest self. Your muse can be a reminder that you are not just someone's mum, someone's partner or someone keeping everything running – you are a whole person with dreams, ambitions and an identity of your own. And the more you embody that energy, the more you attract opportunities, confidence and the life you've been manifesting all along.

It's easy to fall into the trap of watching people whose lives look nothing like yours and wondering why you don't feel inspired. I have definitely fallen victim to this. Scrolling through the morning routines of childless college girls or the perfectly curated date nights of married couples doesn't help me live my best life – it just highlights the differences between their reality and mine. And while there's nothing wrong with admiring people in different life stages, it doesn't always translate into something actionable for me. I can't just drop everything and go on a silent retreat for a week or spend two hours journaling in a sunlit café every morning. My life is full, messy and beautifully chaotic, and I need role models whose lives reflect that. That's why I find real motivation in women whose lives look more like mine: single mothers making things happen, women running businesses while raising kids, those who are building their dreams in the in-between moments of school runs and bedtime stories. Just look at the Kardashian sisters. Every single one of them, bar Kendal, has been or is a single mother and they are killing it! Women in their thirties and forties who are living out loud, dating younger men, travelling and having the time of their lives – those are my muses! Seeing someone thrive *while* juggling responsibilities reminds me that success and joy are still possible, even when life is demanding. It's proof that I don't have to wait for the perfect circumstances to start showing up for myself. Instead of longing for a reality that isn't mine, I focus on role models who make me think, 'If she can do it, so can I.' Because the truth is, we don't need a different life to feel inspired, we just need to see what's possible within the one we already have.

Who are your role models? Who could you look to for inspo while manifesting your dreams? When discovering your muses, try to find people to cover different areas of life. I look for people who I admire in the following areas:

- home and lifestyle
- beauty and style
- career and achievements
- relationship or mothering style

I'm an absolute sucker for an Instagram home account and pore over whimsical cottages with floral archways or exposed brick warehouses in east London. They inspire me and help me put together my own style at home, because we can't all afford an interior designer! It also gives me motivation to keep my house beautiful and organised.

I found that looking for style inspo on short or brunette people simply wasn't working as what suited them often didn't suit me. I found it so helpful to find a couple of influencers or models with the same body type and hair as me. It motivated me to try new styles which looked good on them, and of course it's always important to see yourself represented.

Find people whose career you admire and the path is all laid out for you before your eyes. You're welcome. Whatever it is you want to achieve, there's a formula and, the good news is, someone has done it before you. Find people who have done what you want to do. In my industry of 'the law of attraction', it's incredibly common, if not inevitable, for people to turn to high-end coaching, charging thousands for their services. I started to get disheartened as that wasn't the route I wanted to go down at all. Instead, I found myself career muses outside of my niche who were recording amazing podcasts, writing books and hosting huge events – all without a discovery call in sight.

Social media isn't real, but love is. Find a muse who has the relationship and mothering style you admire and want to replicate in your own life. I bet there are inspirational women out there who pop out a baby, leave it with a nanny then are back to full-time work with a full face of make-up three days after birth looking slim, toned and like nothing happened. This could be absolute goals to one person, but it certainly isn't for me. I seek out women who are rich in time with their children, are able to commit to the demands of attachment parenting and

MANIFEST LIKE A MOTHER

who have freedom in their life to live as they please. Whose relationship do you admire? Which couples seem like they are genuinely best friends as well as life partners? Do you want a golden retriever boyfriend? An Instagram husband? Or maybe it's time to take a one-way ticket to Cougar Town . . . Find what you want and go for it!

This brings me to the most powerful part of the trilogy: dressing for the life you want.

Dressing for the Life You Want

There's a reason writer, designer and speaker Austin Kleon's phrase 'dress for the job you want, not the job you have' is so well known – it speaks to the power of showing up as the version of yourself you're stepping into, not just the one you are today. But this idea isn't just for careers; it applies to every part of our lives, including motherhood and manifestation. The way we dress is an extension of how we see ourselves and, when we put intention into it, it can become a daily practice of stepping into our highest, most magnetic self. Dressing for the life you want isn't about vanity, it's about energy, confidence and aligning with the reality you are calling in.

As a mother, it's easy to fall into the habit of throwing on whatever is quickest and most practical: leggings and an old sweatshirt was my *outfit du jour* for years, but what if the way we dressed wasn't just about convenience, but about stepping into the version of ourselves we're working to become? The way we present ourselves sends a powerful message, not just to the world (who will notice, trust me!), but to our own subconscious. When we take a little extra care in how we dress, even in the smallest ways, we align ourselves with the future we're manifesting. Dressing for the life you want isn't about being unrealistic or impractical – it's about embodying the energy of the woman you are becoming.

As you think about future you, the version of you who has achieved her goals and is living her dream life, what does she look like? Is she on a yacht, sipping champagne with the love of her life in a shitty old swimsuit that's seen better days? Is she launching her new business at a glittering event, wearing old leggings and no make-up? I think it's safe to say, no. When we visualise our future selves, we are usually fit, feeling great and looking fabulous, with a wardrobe to match. Think of it this way: if your dream life involves feeling confident, successful and radiant, why wait until *after* you've 'arrived' to start dressing that way? Even if you're just doing the school run or working from home, putting on something that makes you feel put-together shifts your mindset. I'm the comfort queen and you better believe I'm not changing that for anyone, but even upgrading and being intentional about comfy clothes makes a huge difference.

It's not about spending a fortune on a new wardrobe; it's about making intentional choices. Wearing a beautiful dress, adding a swipe of lipstick or swapping the worn-out loungewear for something that makes you feel elevated can instantly change your energy. When you dress in a way that reflects your future self, you start moving through the world with that version of you in mind – making choices, taking actions and showing up in ways that align with her.

Dressing for the life you want isn't just about clothes – it's a powerful form of both mindfulness and manifestation. It's telling the Universe (and yourself) that you are *already* that woman. You don't have to wait until you have more time, more money or fewer responsibilities to show up for yourself in this way. By making small, intentional shifts in how you dress, you create a ripple effect that spills into every area of your life. You feel more confident, you carry yourself differently and you attract opportunities and experiences that align with your energy. So, tomorrow morning, instead of reaching for what's easiest, ask yourself: 'What would the future me wear today?' And then put it on.

A few years ago in my book club, we spent a month manifesting through the way we dress and present ourselves to the world – and it was enlightening! For me, dressing for the day I intend to have is one of the most powerful forms of mindfulness, as I'm not putting off the best version of me and my best life to someday, it's *today*! I found I had so much more confidence, I talked to people more, I was open to more opportunities and just had more fun. What was interesting was the way people reacted to me too. They were more open, more interested and took me more seriously.

One of the tasks that month was to look at our daily outfits and take mirror selfies, then write down what we saw. What kind of woman was this with the unwashed mum bun in the old leggings and top with baby dribble on? Was she rich or poor? Ambitious or lazy? Interesting or a bore? I realised that even though I knew I was a bad bitch boss woman who had many plates spinning, I presented as a tired, bored woman who didn't take much pride in her appearance. I tend to have two settings: homeless or drag queen, but the problem was, the homeless look was getting 90 per cent of the airtime during this season of motherhood. I guess I was an all-or-nothing kind of a girl, and I noticed that on my child-free jaunts to London – whether it was for the weekend or a day of meetings or recordings – I put the time and effort into my 'lewk' and it paid off. People took me seriously, I was confident, things went well and I was open to opportunities, whether it was a random chat on the train, putting myself forward at an event or, as I mentioned earlier, getting a dick appointment with the restaurant manager.

It was a stark contrast to my 'at-home' attire, for days with the children, bustling through baby groups, food shops and working from home. Although my call for looking good during these activities was much less, I realised how much of an impact trudging through daily life not looking or feeling good was having on me. I would avoid people more, have less confidence in myself, not strike up conversations as much and just generally enjoy life less. As I said before, these mundane, ordinary days make up the majority of our lives, and so it's actually wild that I would spend so little effort on this portion of my life. When I started to make some real changes I saw incredible results – fast!

How to dress for the life you want

Firstly, take a picture of your outfit every morning for a whole week, without changing a thing. Examine your looks with fresh eyes and ask yourself:

- What kind of woman is this?
- What kind of habits does she have?
- What kind of house does she live in?
- What does she do?
- Is she successful?
- Has she got her shit together?
- Does she look approachable?

Next, figure out what kind of woman you want to be. How does she dress? For some, it will be to be a businesswoman in power suits and heels in the city; for others, they crave the whimsical cottage core look and curate an entire identity based on a neutral palette and vintage, natural textures. That's their vibe! For me, when I did this exercise, I wanted my wardrobe to portray that I am an interesting creative and I'm free to live how I want (so no office clothes or business suits for me).

Who do you want to be? Find examples of styles, outfits and people whose fashion sense you love. Before you use this as an excuse to go out shopping, you're going to shop your own closet first. So many of us having wardrobes bursting at the seams yet routinely claim 'I have nothing to wear!' Let's remedy that. Keeping in mind the style you want, go through your entire wardrobe and declutter anything that you haven't worn in a year, that doesn't fit, isn't flattering, isn't comfortable or you simply just don't like.

Studies show that most people wear less than 50 per cent of their wardrobe regularly, meaning the majority of what's hanging in our closets is just taking up space. A cluttered wardrobe not only makes getting dressed more stressful, but also keeps us stuck in versions of ourselves that no longer serve us. Holding on to clothes that don't fit, don't suit us or don't align with the person we're becoming creates unnecessary decision fatigue and can even reinforce limiting beliefs about our bodies or lifestyle. By the way, I'm not suggesting at this point that you channel your inner Simon Cowell and reduce your wardrobe to a collection of identical V-neck T-shirts, jeans and height-boosting heels. By decluttering and keeping only what truly fits, flatters and reflects the energy of the life we're manifesting, we make it easier to step into our highest self every day. A streamlined, intentional wardrobe means clearing space for confidence, ease and alignment with the future we're creating.

Now your wardrobe has been cleaned and cleared, only what you love and what fits should remain. I personally love to do this twice a year when I change over my summer and winter wardrobe. As much as I've tried to ditch the fast fashion and embrace investing in higher quality, intentional pieces, I still seem to attract wardrobe clutter to clear every year!

At this point, you should try on all the pieces you love, styled with different items in combinations you haven't tried before. You will be surprised at how many outfit combinations you can discover without buying a single thing!

Something I read in *Style Therapy* by Lauren Messiah is that you can hack your way to a wardrobe you love by finding outfit formulas that suit you and you can replicate. So, an example for me is that, as a mum in my mid-thirties, I often struggled when going on a night out – what do people even wear anymore?! I discovered through this book that an outfit I tried and loved was a short leather skirt teamed with a casual tee tucked in and flat leopard ankle boots. I wore it on a night out and felt so good, so comfortable but also in alignment with what my style goal was: to portray myself as a successful, interesting creative.

This book taught me that I could not only love this outfit, but that I could break down its formula and replicate it. And so I did. I found a few different variations of the skirt in different fabrics and went on a hunt for a more versatile, black pair of boots in the same style. I now had myself around three or four variations of this look and I *always* had something to wear on a night out!

What outfits do you absolutely love and find yourself going back to over and over again? Can you break that outfit down and replicate the formula to increase the number of outfits in your wardrobe that you love and would wear?

Only once you have fully rediscovered the depths of your own wardrobe should you head out to the shops to fill in any gaps you have with intention.

MANIFEST LIKE A MOTHER

At the heart of all this – romanticising your life, stepping into main character energy and dressing for the life you want – is the simple but powerful truth that you are worthy of joy, beauty and self-celebration right now. Not when the kids are older, not when you're at your goal weight, not when life slows down, not when you've reached some imagined finish line. Every small choice you make to romanticise your daily routine, curate your energy and dress in a way that reflects your future self is an act of self-respect and manifestation in motion. You are the author of your story, the creator of your reality, and the more you show up as the woman you aspire to be, the faster your life begins to align with that vision. The magic isn't in waiting for the perfect moment, it's in choosing to embody it today.

And now we come to the final part of how to manifest like a mother – the secret ingredient that will supercharge all your other goals . . . manifesting *money*! Yes, you are going to channel your inner Oprah as you smash your money blocks, discover what 'rich' means to you and start living rich – right now!

206

Chapter 12

RICH MUM VIBES

'Something I absolutely had to include in this book was the subject of money mindset. Of all the aspects of the law of attraction that I have explored over the years, this has to be my favourite – so I've saved the best till last.'

Something I've noticed over the years is that 'money education', particularly online, is very different for men than it is for women. Men are encouraged to invest, to grow, to expand. Women, for the most part, are told to cut back, save, restrict, even fucking coupon! No thanks love. I remember once watching a TV show (I can't remember what it was, but it was on mainstream TV at primetime) about getting your finances in order for the new year. They got one poor woman to forgo her monthly date night out with her husband and instead cook at home for him. I couldn't help but laugh in terror as she sat there, among her children's toys, as she and her husband got dressed up to eat on their sofa with a single sad candle. *That was their advice!* I don't know about you, but fuck that. I want advice that will expand my possibilities, that will make me *rich*, not recommendations to cut back on the small pleasures I have in life.

For many people, the idea of talking about money, how much you earn, how you earn it, how you spend it, if you're in debt, how much debt you have, if you have savings or investments, or your dreams of what you would do if you were rich are strictly off limits, even to themselves. Talking about money is seen as vulgar, rude and just isn't done – especially here in the UK. I want us to release those limitations now as we go into this chapter with an open mind.

I am so passionate about money mindset for two reasons. Number one is that when you get into manifesting, you really want to believe that you are bringing your goals into reality. Of course, the more you see your goals undoubtedly manifesting into your reality, the more belief you will have for your next goal, and it becomes a powerful self-fulfilling prophecy. When we manifest opportunities, people or signs, it's all very subjective. For example, I could say I want to manifest the love of my life, and then I find some crackhead on Tinder who doesn't have a job and is mean to me, and I'm like, 'Look, I manifested my dream man!' I've seen this happen before. Did we really manifest what we deserve?

With money, it's clear and objective. Just like Shakira's hips, numbers don't lie – you either achieved your money goal or you didn't. For this reason, I love to manifest very *specific* money goals. The first year I ever hosted my little online goal-setting party, I had no idea how many people would buy tickets. It was just me, my ten-year-old MacBook camera and a very rudimentary Facebook group. Tickets were £15 and I set a ridiculous goal of making £44,000. That was how much I used to make in a year! And I thought I could make that in just a couple of hours on one event . . . madness. I made it a very specific number as I wanted to hit it on the head. I didn't round up or down. And, you've guessed it – that first party made just over £44,000. Make your money goal super specific so that when you hit it, you know *you* did that.

Number two is that the majority of my audience are mothers and we all know about the motherhood penalty. The motherhood penalty is a real and frustrating issue that affects so many women financially. Studies show that mums earn significantly less than dads, with research from the Fawcett Society revealing that mothers face a pay gap of around 15 per cent compared to women without children. Over time, this gap adds up, impacting pensions, savings and career progression. A report by the Institute for Fiscal Studies (IFS) found that, by the time their first child is 12, UK mothers earn 33 per cent less per hour than fathers, largely due to the pressure to take on part-time work or step back from their careers.

This isn't just about pay – it's about opportunities too. Research from the Trades Union Congress (TUC) shows that mothers are far more likely to be in insecure work, with less access to promotions and pay rises. And let's not forget the cost of childcare, which is so high in the UK that many women find it's simply not worth working full-time. All of this leaves mothers at a financial disadvantage, often making them more reliant on partners, struggling to build financial independence and definitely not living their best lives. It's a broken system and we can try to change it, but while we're waiting for that to happen, we can do something which is quite fun – get rich. As a mother, becoming my own version of rich has bought me so much: time with my girls, childcare so I can work on my dream career, incredible experiences all over the world, a dreamy environment in which to raise my children, ease, joy, protection, choices and freedom. I think that's the most important one: freedom.

What would more money give you the freedom to do? Leave a toxic partner? Live in your own home rather than at the mercy of your dickhead landlord? Homeschool your children? Privately educate them? Stay home to raise your children? Send your children to boarding school so you don't have to see them? Afford childcare so you could pursue your dreams? Pack up and take your family on an adventure around the world? Flex on these hoes with a Ferrari? There's no right answer here, but allow yourself to be completely honest.

Money has absolutely transformed my life and my mother-hood, and I want that for you too.

A Set Income Does Not Exist

The first idea I want you to get your head around is that there is no such thing as a 'set income'. It simply does not exist. So if you are reading this, thinking this doesn't apply to me, I'm a full-time teacher, I'm a stay-at-home mum, I'm the President of Namibia (hello Netumbo!), then I'm here to call *bullshit*! A set income does not exist – say it with me: 'A set income does not exist!'

When I look back on my own humble life, there were never any limits.

As a school child of 12, I had a dog-walking business and washed glasses in a pub at the weekends. That enabled me to buy my first pony!

At my first full-time job in London as a very bad PA, I had side hustles including eBaying designer clothes for my rich friends (was I the Kim Kardashian of north London? Yes), writing real-life features and doing copy-writing for online fashion retailers.

As a newly single mum with a full-on schedule of baby-raising and working in my salon, I did Airbnb on the side, leveraging my space when I was no longer able to leverage my time.

In the lockdown when salons were closed, I started a pod-cast and sold candles and manifesting boxes from home.

The examples are endless and this is just me. I hope that you can see that even if you do have a full-time job or you don't work, that doesn't exclude you from windfalls, business ideas, entrepreneurship, investments, side hustles and so much more.

A concept I learnt a few years ago in a book amazingly titled *Rich As F*ck*, was that we all carry with us energetic set points of how much and how little we will allow ourselves to either earn or have. Your energetic set point around money is like an internal thermostat – it regulates how much wealth you allow yourself to accumulate, no matter what's happening externally. You might get a pay rise, land a big new client or receive unexpected money, but if your subconscious beliefs are stuck at a lower financial set point, that extra cash will somehow disappear. Maybe you'll suddenly have a big expense, donate more than you intended or feel the urge to splurge it away. On the flip side, if your set point is higher, you'll naturally attract and hold on to more money because your mind expects it.

Have you experienced this in your own life? Think of a time when you got an extra income stream, a pay rise or, conversely, an unexpected extra bill each month. It eventually just evens back out again. It's for this reason that I always push myself a little when getting a mortgage to go a bit above what I am comfortable paying. I know that within a few months my disposable income will match what it was before the housing upgrade. (That's *not* financial advice, by the way, but it works for me!)

This concept of always returning to your energetic base-line is why some people seem to always be broke, no matter how much they earn, while others keep growing their wealth with ease. It's not just about income; it's about identity. If deep down you see yourself as someone who gets by rather than someone who thrives financially, your actions will always bring you back to that familiar place. Do you want the good news? Of course you do! You can raise your energetic set point by consistently affirming new beliefs, surrounding yourself with wealth-conscious influences and acting as the version of you who naturally holds and enjoys financial abundance. The goal is to make more money feel normal for you, so instead of sabotaging financial success, you start expanding into it.

I would love for you to think about what your energetic minimums and maximums are. To give you an idea, back when I started this money mindset exploration a few years ago, my minimum was about £200 overdrawn but no debt and my maximum was about £3,000 with no savings. It didn't matter what new venture I explored or how much more I spent, it always resettled back to this.

Simply acknowledging that there is no such thing as a set income and being aware of your own energetic minimum and maximum is incredibly powerful.

The next idea designed to expand your capabilities for abundance is . . .

Your Self-Worth = Your Net Worth

The more worthy you feel, the more you will increase your net worth. This isn't just about earning more money, it's about what you believe you deserve. We talked about this earlier in the book, regarding what you are able to manifest into your life, and it's just as true for money.

Women, in particular, have been conditioned to put themselves last, to downplay their successes and to feel guilty for wanting financial abundance. But the truth is, your financial reality is a reflection of your self-worth. When you start seeing yourself as someone who is valuable, capable and deserving, you begin to make different choices. You negotiate for higher pay, you stop undercharging, you invest in yourself without guilt and you step into opportunities with confidence.

Money flows to those who expect it, who feel comfortable

receiving it and who trust themselves to handle it. If you've ever found yourself hesitating to ask for a raise, feeling guilty about charging what you're worth or underestimating your value, it's a sign your self-worth and net worth are out of alignment. The key isn't just in learning financial strategies, it's in rewiring your beliefs. Start acting like a Wealthy Woman who is worthy of financial freedom. Speak to yourself with kindness, set boundaries around your time and energy, and remind yourself daily that wealth isn't just for other people – it's for you too, bitch! The more you embrace this, the more you'll see your financial world expand to match it.

A great way to feel worthy of more money is to feel good about money. Two ways I love to do this are:

Get familiar with your finances

One of the best ways to increase your income and improve your money mindset is to actually get to know your money. So many women avoid looking at their finances because of fear, shame or just not wanting to deal with it, and I know because I'm one of them! If you truly want to attract more, you have to show that you can handle what you already have. Money loves clarity, and when you know exactly how much is coming in, going out and where it's all going, you start to feel more in control. That confidence sends a powerful message to the Universe: I am ready for more.

When I first discovered manifesting in my early twenties, I was way too scared to manifest lots of money, justifying it with the fact that I would be scared of huge tax bills and even that I wouldn't want the maintenance of a big house. I literally told the Universe I didn't want it. It was only once I worked on my money mindset and overcame these blocks I was able to manifest lots of money. I got the big house with the building and gardens to maintain and it wasn't the big scary monster I thought it would be. I also had my worst fear come true, which I'm very thankful for. After a couple of years of success with the podcast, overpaying on my mortgages like a madwoman and keeping a team of builders in work for over a year, I was hit with a £500,000 tax bill. It knocked my money mindset and confidence for six and, if I'm honest, I still wasn't familiar with my finances. It was all for the greater good though, as I exceeded levels of wealth I had never experienced before. Soon, I was able to see that I needed to walk through my worst fear and, you know what, I survived it.

None of my friends could really relate to this kind of problem and when I said I had a £500,000 tax bill they would exclaim in horror that I should just shut up shop and go bankrupt. That put even more fear into me! Instead, I had to get inspo from a documentary about footballers who are all young men, mostly from working class backgrounds who suddenly come into *lots* of money, just like I did. As I heard case after case of these men not always having the best advice and having to readjust to this level of wealth, often with surprise tax bills along the way, I realised it was somewhat of a rite of passage. I resolved to use it as a lesson, upgrade my money mindset yet again and move on.

A great exercise to build this awareness is to track your money daily for a month. Every single day, write down any money that comes into your life – your salary, business income, benefits, gifts, refunds, even finding a £5 note on the street. Do the same for your expenses, writing down where your money is going. This isn't about restriction or judgement, it's simply about awareness. By the end of the month, you'll have a clear picture of your finances, and you'll likely notice patterns, opportunities to increase your income or areas where you're spending in ways that don't align with your goals. This simple habit not only helps you manage your money better, but also shifts your mindset from scarcity to abundance. The more you pay attention to money, the more money pays attention to you.

Practise aligned spending

The second way I like to increase my worthiness when it comes to making more money is to clarify if I am spending in alignment with my goals and values. When you think back to the most memorable and joyful moments in your life, what stands out for you? Is it the spontaneous adventures, the laughter with friends or maybe the feeling of driving a car that turns heads? For me, I think about when I first quit my corporate job of 15 years and was able to walk my dog through the streets of London in the midday sunshine wearing jeans, flip-flops and, to be honest, whatever the hell I wanted. I went to meet my friend for lunch in the square mile, my old stomping ground, and what I noticed most was how she was limited to just an hour in a dingy pub, wearing sensible black office clothes, wrapped up despite the midday sun as it was obvious her office, like mine used to be, was set to a chilly 18°C. This used to be me; there's no such thing as dressing seasonally when it's always freezing in your office! As I walked home after that lunch, I couldn't believe how free I felt, being able to wear what I wanted and enjoy the weather. *That* was a formative memory for me and I realised that my freedom was my number-one value.

Another moment that stands out to me is walking on the beach in Barbados with my friend Kelly and my daughters, slightly drunk on rosé wine if I'm honest, watching the sun set and running in and out of the waves as the girls screamed in delight. I felt such elation to be able to experience this beautiful part of the world with my little family. That's when I realised how much I also valued fun and adventure.

What do you value most?

I invite you to think about some of the most joyful and memorable moments in your life. These are the experiences that hold the most meaning, right? Now, take a moment to reflect on how you're spending your money. Does it align with these values, whether it's adventure, family, material possessions, personal growth or creativity? If your spending habits aren't supporting the things that truly light you up, it's time to reassess. Money is a tool that should work in harmony with your deepest values and desires, not against them. If your spending is out of sync with your true goals, the Universe won't feel confident entrusting you with more.

When I discovered I had a £500,000 tax bill, my accountants and I did a lot of reflection and a little bit of crying. The crying was more me, to be fair; I don't think Steve and John lost any sleep. I was so pleased to discover that the vast majority of the spending had been on purchasing my dream home, making it the perfect place to raise my daughters and overpaying on the mortgage to the point where if I had kept going for another two years, it would have been entirely paid off. Although me not being 100 per cent clear on my finances had got me into that situation, I'm so happy that the money that was spent didn't go on designer clothes, flashy cars, trying to keep up with the Joneses . . . you get the idea. The knowledge that it had gone on creating a stable family home made paying that bill an actual enjoyable experience – yes, really! It's also the reason why I've been able to bounce back from it, because that experience tells me that I am able to trust myself, even when I get into a bit of a mess. My intentions are good and my spending is in alignment.

Money is energy, and energy follows alignment. If you're spending on things that don't make you feel good or bring you closer to the life you want, then you'll probably resist more abundance because you don't truly believe you deserve it or think that it's going to make your life worse. Imagine if as a single woman getting richer, you found you only attracted men who wanted to sponge off you and you allowed it. That feeling of being used would be so low vibrational, it would actually repel money in the future.

To attract more wealth, start by aligning your spending with your passions and values, then watch as the Universe responds, offering opportunities, growth and financial abundance. When money aligns with your purpose, that's when the magic happens.

Honour Your Money

This seems a good segue into honouring your money, which is another fabulous way to increase your income. Honouring your money means treating it with the respect and care it deserves. Just as we honour our time, health and relationships, we should do the same with our finances. It starts with being mindful of how we manage and care for the money that flows in and out of our lives. If you love, appreciate and take care of the money you already have, the Universe will give you more.

This can be as simple as looking at your subscriptions and direct debits – are there any you've forgotten about or no longer use? Cancelling those unnecessary payments is a great first step, no matter how small they seem. Take the time to return items you no longer want or need, freeing up space in your life (and your finances). Again, it's about being intentional with every penny, making sure your spending aligns with your values and priorities.

Practical steps like keeping your purse clean and clutter-free is a favourite of mine – cutting up old redundant cards, throwing out receipts and unscrunching your cash can make a surprising difference. When your purse is tidy, it creates a sense of order and control over your money.

Don't forget about saving. Even small amounts can add up, and building savings is a form of respecting your financial future. The key is not to restrict, but to make thoughtful, conscious decisions about how you handle your money daily. Every time you honour your finances by decluttering, saving, hiring an accountant or making good decisions, you're telling the Universe you're ready for more abundance. This practice can shift your mindset, allowing you to attract more wealth and create a healthier relationship with money.

Release Money-Limiting Beliefs

Overcoming money blocks and limiting beliefs is a powerful step towards opening up the flow of abundance into your life. These blocks can show up in so many forms: fear of success, a belief that you don't deserve wealth or the idea that money is hard to come by. For example, as a single woman, I have a die-hard belief that the richer or more successful I become, the harder it becomes to meet a man. Luckily, that block so far has only blocked men from my life, not money – ha ha!

It's important to remember that each time you release a limiting belief or block, you create more space for abundance to flow freely into your life. As you work through these blocks, visualise that flow of money and opportunities expanding – imagine the energy of abundance opening up to you, just waiting to come into your life.

The first step in breaking through money blocks is, as always, decluttering. Start by clearing both the physical and mental space around you. This could mean tidying up your workspace, whether that's your desktop or your literal desk, clearing out old receipts or donating things that you were going to sell or return but never got around to. The act of decluttering is symbolic of clearing mental and emotional space. A tidy environment can help you feel more in control, open and receptive to new opportunities. As you declutter, imagine the space you're creating in your life being filled with abundance and new possibilities.

One of the most important steps in overcoming money blocks is simply identifying the limiting beliefs that have been holding you back. These beliefs often stem from past experiences, cultural conditioning or fears that we've inherited over time. Becoming aware of our limiting beliefs is so important because they sneak into our lives without us having any idea – just like when you go and stay with a friend's family when you're a teen and you realise that not every family is like yours and that what's 'normal' to you is completely different for somebody else.

I inherited both good and bad money beliefs from my family. I was taught that you should never get into debt, use store cards, credit cards or even car finance. This has served me *pretty* well, meaning that I have always comfortably lived within my means and never got into credit card debt. Living within my means as a non-negotiable has meant that I have always felt rich, no matter how much I've earned. Thanks Mum! However, as I've got older, I've had to question the credit card part as everyone around me was taking advantage of Amex/BA air miles except me! I made the heady decision, in my mid-thirties, to take out an American Express card and put what I could on there to add up my points. After just a year or so of doing this and paying it off in full each month, I got myself a pretty much gratis return flight to the Bahamas for my birthday – oi oi!

My mum and nan also taught me that renting was a mug's game. They encouraged me and my sister from a really early age to save, save, save and buy, buy, buy. Although, again, this has served me well as I bought my first London property in my late twenties on a pretty small salary while my friends were priced out of the rental market one by one, I also went against their advice and spent the first half of my twenties house sharing (renting!) in Camden with some incredible people. I wouldn't trade those years living in my house share for anything.

My parents also made me believe I had to take a nine-to-five job and stick with it until I died, depressed from a lifetime of a shitty, dead-end job. It was because of this that I spent the majority of my twenties stuck in an office job and lifestyle I loathed. Not once did they suggest that I could do something different with my life, and I don't know if I was dim, but despite my numerous side hustles, it just didn't seem to be an option for me. It was only when I met my ex-husband that he convinced me to quit the job I hated and embrace the freedom I craved, being a self-employed entrepreneur.

Your money-limiting beliefs may look completely different to mine. It could be that men don't like rich, successful women, that working in the hair and beauty industry is tiring and has a ceiling income, that women who look like you can never make it in the corporate world or that making money is extremely difficult. Maybe your belief could be that capitalism is wrong, rich people are evil, poor people are lazy or anything in between.

The first step is to acknowledge these beliefs, examine where they came from and then replace them with new, empowering thoughts that serve your goals. This is where the true transformation happens, because as you shift these beliefs, you shift your energy and your results.

Let's start with an example: one common limiting belief is, 'Money is hard to come by'. If you find yourself thinking this, take a moment to ask where it originated. Did you hear it growing up? Was it hard for your family to make money? Do you associate money with struggle? Once you've recognised it, reframe it. Instead of thinking, 'Money is hard to come by', shift the thought to, 'Money flows to me easily when I take inspired action'. This new thought is more empowering and opens you up to receiving wealth without the struggle. If that affirmation feels too much of a leap, simply look around at the countless examples of how much money is flowing to other people, just like you. Today, more than ever, ordinary people are getting rich. Like, really rich.

If you have the common limiting belief 'I'll never be able to manage my money properly', it's time to shift that perspective. Everyone can learn to manage money more effectively with the right knowledge and habits. This is a particular belief that kept me playing small for *years*. Reframe the belief to, 'I am capable of managing my money wisely, and I am continuously learning and improving'. This empowers you to take action and seek the tools and resources that will help you develop your financial skills, one at a time.

As I went from being an employee making £21k a year to a self-employed bad bitch owning a corporation turning over tens of thousands of pounds per month, I had to make incremental upgrades to my mindset, my processes and my life. It started with hiring a bookkeeper, right through to having a team of people working with me to manage it all. It can totally be done, slowly but surely.

Busting beliefs

As you go through each limiting belief, take the time to write down what you're thinking, then consciously choose a new, empowering belief to replace it. Each time a limiting thought arises, acknowledge it and immediately reframe it into something positive. It may take time to shift old patterns, but remember, the more you practise this, the easier it becomes.

The process of reframing not only releases the negative energy tied to the belief, but it also invites new, positive energy to flow into your life, aligning you with the abundance that is already available to you.

By working through each limiting belief with this method, you create a new mindset, one that is open to receiving abundance and aligned with the wealth and success you deserve. Visualise your new beliefs manifesting into reality as you continue working through your money blocks – each shift you make opens the door to more opportunities, more money and more fulfilment.

Something I love to do when I am trying to release money blocks and allow myself to embrace a new level of wealth is to surround myself with money. Now, I don't mean lying naked on a bed of cash (although I did once do that in my mid-twenties with a slightly dodgy guy I was dating, but that's a story for another book). What I mean is, I immerse myself in proof of wild, obscene wealth.

I love to watch TV shows that demonstrate just how much money is out there. Shows that focus on high-end real estate agents show you that there are numerous people out there buying up property in a city near you for millions upon millions of pounds. These people aren't royalty or even famous – they're regular people with a shit tonne of money. I love to watch *The Kardashians* for this same reason. I will always remember a particular episode where Kris Jenner forgot about an entire condo she owned. Like, she just forgot.

Recently, Khloé and Kim went to a wedding in India for the Ambani family and wow – the level of wealth was wild. The Ambani family is one of the wealthiest in the world. Mukesh Ambani had a net worth of approximately $120 billion as of July 2024, making him the richest person in Asia. In July 2024, Anant Ambani, Mukesh's youngest son, married Radhika Merchant in a lavish ceremony in Mumbai. The wedding was a multi-day event attended by numerous celebrities. The total cost of the wedding was estimated to be around $600 million.

Now, I'm not saying that spending $600 million on a wedding is desirable – of course it's not – but the goal here is to show you the vast amount of money out there. All of a sudden, doubling your income doesn't seem so crazy, does it?

So whether it's super-rich dynasties, billionaire boys in Dubai, girls making millions on OnlyFans or spoilt housewives living a life of luxury, it really doesn't matter if it's your bag, it simply shows you what is out there and what is possible. There are so many TV shows about businesses and brands that were built from the ground up and I can't get enough of them. They motivate and inspire me – so find something that can be your money muse.

Now, surround yourself with positivity

This includes curating your environment, both physically and mentally. Surround yourself with people who uplift you, people who are aligned with the energy of abundance. We don't all have a bunch of wealthy, successful pals to hang out with all day, so you can improvise with who you hang out with 'virtu-ally'. The books you read, the podcasts you listen to, the social media accounts you follow – they should all inspire you to believe in your ability to create wealth. The more you immerse yourself in positivity, the more likely you are to stay focused and motivated.

Then, take inspired action

Manifestation isn't just about wishing for things then sitting back watching *This Morning* waiting for it to all happen. It's about taking deliberate, inspired steps towards your goals. This could mean researching new income streams, taking a course to upskill, hiring a bookkeeper or setting financial goals with clear action steps. Every time you take action, you are signalling to the Universe that you are ready and willing to receive what you've asked for. Action turns your vision into reality, and it is one of the most powerful ways to shift your mindset from scar-city to abundance. Ever noticed how you only feel stressed about something (and that could include money) when you're just passively worrying about it but not taking action towards solving it? The action is incredibly powerful.

Finally, receive and repeat

This is often the hardest part, especially if you've struggled with money blocks for a long time. It's important to recog-nise and accept the abundance that starts to show up in your life. Whether it's a pay rise, a new opportunity or even small blessings like finding money on the street, acknowledge it with gratitude. The more you allow yourself to receive, the more the Universe will send your way. After you've completed this process, repeat it regularly. Continue clearing blocks, taking action and embracing abundance. This cycle will reinforce your belief in your ability to create wealth and keep the flow of abundance wide open.

One thing I have experienced as I have worked on my money mindset over the last few years is that the old saying 'New level, new devil' is so true! You may think that as you do the work and increase your income, you will not be afflicted with money blocks anymore, but the truth is that they just change. They're different. I used to have limiting beliefs about being a single mother and that people would judge me for not having clean windows or my grass cut, but as I became the wealthiest bitch in town I had *new* limiting beliefs that people would think I was wasteful, making my home as beautiful and comfortable as I could. The truth is, I don't think anyone gave a shit and it was all in my head.

As you work through each block using this formula, remember that every step you take is moving you closer to the life you desire. Increase your energetic set points one tax bracket at a time!

Try On Your Dream Life for Size

Often, we struggle with money blocks because we haven't clearly defined our goals. It's vital to know exactly what you want when it comes to your finances. Be specific: what does being rich mean to you? We will all come up with a different amount that will enable us to feel free. Do you want to buy a house, invest in your children's education, buy a fabulous set of new tits or increase your income by a certain amount? Write it down.

Go one better by finding out exactly how much all these things cost. I often find, when shopping with a budget bigger than I've had before, I'm a little unclear on what is available to me. So find out exactly how much what you want to buy is going to cost you. Otherwise, how can you hit a target you can't see?

Back when I wanted to buy my dream house to raise my children in, I had never shopped at the top end of the market in my area before. All my life, whether it was buying my flat in London or my little house here in the country, I was looking at the bottom, cheapest 2–4 per cent of properties in the area. Now, I had to understand what I could get at the top! I went to view house after house, gauging exactly how much space I wanted and the money I needed to spend. It was only after extensively looking at an exclusive luxury development in my village that I decided they were overpriced and with very little garden space. If I hadn't gone to explore them in person I would never have known.

You might have a dream of owning a certain car or a vision of your child attending a particular school. One of the most powerful things you can do for your money mindset right now is to go and experience that dream first-hand. Book the test drive. Attend the open day. When you take inspired action like this, one of two things will happen: you'll either realise it's not actually what you want and you can refine your vision or budget, or you'll feel so inspired and aligned with your dream that it will accelerate your manifestation. Either way, you'll be moving forward with clarity and confidence. This clarity is like setting a compass for your energy, giving you direction and purpose as you move forward.

Release Money with Joy!

A great part of money mindset work that I really enjoy isn't about the money coming in, it's about how we handle the money going out. Think about it: how do you *feel* when you pay your council tax, nursery fees or fork out for new school shoes to replace the ones that your child *literally just* grew out of? If you feel a pang of annoyance, frustration or even resentment every time you spend money on the things that support your life, that's where the shift needs to happen.

Let's say you're paying for a cleaner once a week to help keep your home from descending into total chaos. If you resent that direct debit every time it leaves your account, even though it buys you sanity, space and time with your children, that's a block. The energy you're attaching to that money is negative, so it's no surprise if money starts to feel tight or uncomfortable. On the flip side, when you spend with gratitude – when you say, 'Thank you that I get to invest in support that helps me be a calmer, better mum and *bonus*, I don't have to clean the toilet!' – you're signalling to the Universe that you trust money to come, go and return multiplied.

It's the same with boring bills. The electricity that powers your kettle for your seventeenth cup of tea? The water that fills your child's bath every night? That's money well spent. Try this little mindset switch: next time you make a payment, imagine *not* having that product or service. I find this works best when applied to basic utilities like electricity, gas or water, even your car. Try saying 'thank you' either out loud or in your head: 'Thank you for the warmth, for the nourishment, for the help.' This not only shifts your vibration but also softens your nervous system and, when your body is in a state of safety, it's so much easier to receive.

If you're holding on to money so tightly that it feels like your fists are permanently clenched, you're closing off the flow of abundance. Money loves purpose. It loves movement. And it *really* loves being treated with respect and gratitude. So the next time you catch yourself bitching about a payment, pause and ask: 'How is this serving me or my family?' The answer might surprise you and open you up to receiving so much more.

Poor no more

I would love for you to choose just one thing that makes you feel poor and take immediate action to remedy it. Could it be replacing a broken door handle that falls off every single day? Maybe your underwear that is full of holes. For me, as I write this, I realise that I am still very, very tight on childcare. Firstly, because it makes me feel guilty, but also because, apparently, I enjoy struggling through life. This is quite unlike me to do, but I paused here to call my lovely local childminder and asked her to take the girls out tomorrow for a fun day out while I finish this book. I just gifted myself some space, ease and also a nicer, more relaxed downtime with my girls. I instantly feel *richer*!

Let People Pay You

So you've worked on your money mindset, smashed your limiting beliefs to shit, got clear on your money goals and have had some amazing ideas for how to increase your income . . . now what? Now you have to take the action needed for people to actually pay you. This may sound very obvious, but let me give you an example.

Back when I first started doing my podcast, I didn't really make much, if any, money from it. One evening I was sitting at my sister Anouska's house, talking about what each of us were up to, and she'd just had a meeting in London cancelled with a PR agency that was going to pair up her candle-making business with some celebrity names. All of a sudden, we had an idea to collaborate and create manifesting candles. The ideas started to flow thick and fast – I would name each one after something you would want to manifest so, 'This smells like my future husband', 'This smells like my dream house' and 'This smells like my new baby' – you get the vibe.

We could have talked about this for months and planned and budgeted and so on, but where would that have got us? Instead, I took immediate, imperfect action. My sister had a stock image of the candle vessel we would use – a sleek black glass. So, I called my friend John and asked him if he could design a label and mock up an image of what the label would look like on the candles. He whipped up both in under an hour.

In the meantime, I set up a free e-commerce site on Big Cartel. Now, I'm a basic bitch technophobe and I was still able to set this up and connect it to my PayPal account in less than an hour. Later that night, with zero stock or a single candle made up, I launched it on my Instagram and we took about 400 orders in that first night alone!

Anouska and I were forced into immediate action – her buying up supplies, me getting the perfect labels printed. We made such great money from that venture and continued making the candles for several years after. I had done all the energetic work to be in a great headspace to accept wealth, but I also took the very real action of letting people pay me.

Now you have done the work and got your ideas, how do people actually pay you? Don't ask your friends on Facebook whether they know anyone who wants to rent your spare room, put it on Airbnb to reach people who are looking for a room and will pay you. Don't share photos of your crafts on your Instagram, get them listed on Etsy where people can pay you. Don't ask your followers if they would potentially work with you, make a booking link and put it out there. Let people pay you.

When you open yourself up to receiving – truly receiving – you make it easy for the Universe to deliver. You've done the inner work. You've raised your vibe, got clear on your goals and maybe even written down the number that you'd love to earn. But unless there's a clear and open channel for that abundance to arrive, it simply can't flow. This isn't about waiting around for magic to strike – it's about meeting the Universe halfway.

So, let this be your reminder: don't hide behind planning. Don't wait until it's perfect. Don't keep your gifts quietly tucked away hoping someone stumbles across them. Make it obvious. Make it easy. Make it irresistible. Let people pay you. Because you're ready. And because you're worth it.

Here's the thing – no one is coming to save you. Not the lottery win, not the rich husband, not the long-lost relative with a secret fortune. (And if they are – fabulous, manifest it – but don't wait around for it.) The person you've been waiting for to swoop in and change your financial future? She's already here. Bitch, it's *you*.

You are the magic. You are the abundance. You are the one with the ideas, the energy, the ability to shift everything – not just for yourself, but for your family, your legacy and the generations that follow. That next-level version of yourself? The wealthy, grounded, confident woman who treats money with respect and lets it flow to her easily? She's not a stranger – she's just waiting for you to stop doubting and start stepping into her shoes.

So take the leap. Start tracking your money, raising your worth, letting people pay you and enjoying the hell out of the process. Because the moment you stop waiting for a miracle and realise *you* are the miracle, everything starts to shift. You've got this. Let's go.

Final Word

MANIFEST LIKE A MOTHER

'You've made it! You've read this book, probably in stolen moments between school runs, snack demands and trying to remember what the hell you walked into the kitchen for. But you made it here, and I want you to take a minute to really *celebrate* that because do you know how hard that is when you have the constant demands for attention, not just from your children but from social media and Netflix?'

Taking the time and space to read this book and improve your life is a real boss bitch move and I'm proud of you. You're not the same woman you were when you opened the book to page one. You've started remembering who you are underneath the laundry piles, lunch boxes and late-night googling of toddler sleep regressions.

This book was never about giving you *more* to do. It was about waking something up inside you – a dormant part that has always known you were made for more. More joy. More freedom. More abundance. More magic. And guess what? You don't have to wait until the children are grown up or your house is spotless or you finally feel 'ready'. Manifesting is not reserved for those who have time to sit cross-legged for eight hours a day in a silent retreat in Bali. It's for you – the mum in the leggings covered in baby vom, that bitch running on caffeine and chaos, the woman holding everyone else together but finally, finally deciding to choose herself too.

We've talked about how understanding and working with your menstrual cycle can become your superpower, how everyday mum routines can become self-care rituals and how your home can become your greatest ally in achieving your biggest goals. We've reframed chores as meditations, turned crafts with the kids into vision board sessions and discovered that your wardrobe can be a portal to your future self. We've tackled money mindset, kicked limiting beliefs in the ball bag and opened the floodgates to abundance – now, *swim in it*!

As we close this final chapter, I want you to remember some-thing very important: nobody is coming to save you. That's not a sad realisation after one too many nights on Tinder – it's the most liberating realisation you'll ever have. Because *you* are the person you've been waiting for. You are the magic. When you realise that, when you own it, you become *dangerously* power-ful. A wise woman named Tamu Thomas once said to me, 'Your children don't need a martyr – they need a role model.' They need a mum who shows them what it is to really live. A mum who is lit up, in her power, having fun, prioritising peace and living her best goddamn life.

So, what does it really mean to *Manifest Like a Mother*?

It means showing up – tits leaking, hair messy, hands full, eyes blurry, but with unwavering commitment to your dreams. It means casting spells between the school run and the bedtime chaos, infusing your intentions into the never-ending nappy changes, packed lunches and lullabies. It's about weaving your wildest desires into the fabric of everyday family life – not waiting for quiet or perfection, but claiming your right to dream big in the middle of the madness.

It's finding the sacred in the mundane and knowing that,

every moment, no matter how ordinary, holds the power to reconnect you to your vision. It's choosing to believe that your dreams matter just as much as anyone else's – even when they're currently buried under laundry piles and drowned out by another fucking episode of *PAW Patrol*.

Your next level doesn't demand perfection, it only asks for your *participation*. So participate, as often as you can, as imperfectly as you're able to. Make it automatic to start showing up for your dreams as naturally as you show up for the demands of everyone else. When doubt creeps in – and it will – remind yourself that you are not just raising babies, you're raising future adults and you're showing them what to expect from this big, beautiful life. Show them what it is to love and value yourself, protect your peace and settle for nothing less than your wildest dreams.

It's time, bitch. Time to expand. Time to create the life you *know* is waiting for you – one goal, one intention, one decision, one slightly frazzled action at a time. That, my friend, is how you manifest like a mother.

References

Chapter 1: The Law of Attraction

Doran, G. T. (1981). There's a SMART way to write management's goals and objectives. *Journal of Management Review, 70*(11), 35–6.

Wigle, R. (17 Jan. 2025). Neurosurgeon explains non-woo-woo way to scientifically manifest your goals: 'There is no magic here'. *New York Post*. Retrieved from https://nypost.com/2025/01/17/health/neurosurgeon-explains-how-to-manifest-your-goals-with-science/.

Chapter 2: Your Motherhood Era

Alderfer, R. (3 Apr. 2024). Just the beginning: Matrescence & maternal health. Intrinsic. Retrieved from https://www.intrinsic.us/post/understanding-matrescence.

Liedloff, J. (1989). *The Continuum Concept: In Search of Happiness Lost* (Penguin).

Chapter 3: Going with the Flow (Literally)

Atukorala, K. R., Silva, W., Amarasiri, L. and Fernando, D. M. S. (2022). Changes in serum testosterone during the menstrual cycle – an integrative systematic review of published literature. *Gynecological and Reproductive Endocrinology & Metabolism, 3*, 9–20.

Beck, T. (9 Aug. 2012). Estrogen and female anxiety. *The Harvard Gazette*. Retrieved from https://news.harvard.edu/gazette/story/2012/08/estrogen-and-female-anxiety/.

Better Health Channel (2 Aug. 2024). Ovulation pain. Retrieved from https://www.betterhealth.vic.gov.au/health/conditionsandtreatments/ovulation-pain.

Enviroliteracy Team. (25 March. 2025.) What is the red tent period? Retrieved from https://enviroliteracy.org/what-is-the-red-tent-period/

Moreland OB-GYN (15 Aug. 2023). Understanding the four phases of the menstrual cycle [blog]. Retrieved from https://www.morelandobgyn.com/blog/4-phases-of-the-menstrual-cycle.

Roberts, S. C., Havlicek, J., Flegr, J., Hruskova, M., Little, A. C., Jones, B. C., Perrett, D. I. and Petrie, M. (7 August. 2004.) Female facial attractiveness increases during the fertile phase of the menstrual cycle. *Proceedings of the Royal Society of London. Series B: Biological Sciences, 271*(suppl_5), S270–2.

Sanchez, M.-T. (n.d.). Women's second body clock: How it works and how to make the most of it [blog]. Women's Brain Foundation. Retrieved from https://www.womensbrainproject.com/2021/03/01/womens-second-body-clock-how-it-works-and-how-to-make-the-most-of-it/.

University of California – Los Angeles (22 Jun. 2007). Putting feelings into words produces therapeutic effects in the brain. ScienceDaily. Retrieved from https://www.sciencedaily.com/releases/2007/06/070622090727.htm.

Chapter 4: An Environment for Success

Fifty Two Hundred Photo (n.d.). Displaying family photos boosts children's self-esteem. Retrieved from

https://www.fiftytwohundredphoto.com/blog/
barnes-family-raleigh-family-photography.

Kondo, M. (2014). *The Life-Changing Magic of Tidying* (Vermilion).

Larbi, D. (2025). *Frequently Happy: 52 Mindful Moments to Bring Hope and Joy* (Rider).

Vujovic, M., Hernández-Leo, D., Tassani, S. and Spikol, D. (2020). Round or rectangular tables for collaborative problem solving? A multimodal learning analytics study. *British Journal of Educational Technology, 51*(5), 1597–614.

Chapter 5: Space to Manifest

Duffield-Thomas, D. (2018). *Get Rich, Lucky Bitch!* (Hay House UK).

Gallagher, K. (2024). *The Goddess Path* (Rider).

Chapter 6: Chore Therapy

Biali Haas, S. (21 Jun. 2019). Working with your hands does wonders for your brain. *Psychology Today*. Retrieved from https://www.psychologytoday.com/us/blog/prescriptions-for-life/201906/working-with-your-hands-does-wonders-for-your-brain.

Conner (8 Aug. 2017). Love is the new super-food. Modern Mediterranean. Retrieved from https://modernmediterranean.com/2017/08/08/love-is/.

Creighton University Libraries (12 Nov. 2024). Time management: Pomodoro technique. Retrieved from https://culibraries.creighton.edu/reading-room/time-management.

Doing Good Together (n.d.). Raising helpful, responsible kids begins with chores. Retrieved from https://www.doinggoodtogether.org/dgt-newsletter/helpful-kids-chores.

Gallagher, K. (2024). *The Goddess Path* (Rider).

Nerem, R. M., Levesque, M. J. and Cornhill, J. F., 1980. Social environment as a factor in diet-induced atherosclerosis. *Science, 208*(4451), 1475–6.

Reich-Stiebert, N., Froehlich, L. and Voltmer, J. B., 2023. Gendered mental labor: A systematic literature review on the cognitive dimension of unpaid work within the household and childcare. *Sex Roles*, *88*(11), 475–94.

Selig, M. (12 Aug. 2022). 8 surprising psychological benefits of routine daily tasks. *Psychology Today*. Retrieved from https://www.psychologytoday.com/us/blog/changepower/202208/8-surprising-psychological-benefits-of-routine-daily-tasks.

Chapter 7: Master Your Week, Master Your Life

@jenlynnbarnes (23 Jan. 2020). One time, I was at a Q&A with Nora Roberts, and someone asked her how to balance writing and kids . . . X. Retrieved from https://x.com/jenlynnbarnes/status/1220182162118451200.

Beverley, G. (2022). *Working Hard, Hardly Working: How to Achieve More, Stress Less and Feel Fulfilled* (Penguin).

Bratslavsky, E., Muraven, M. and Tice, D. M. (1998). Ego depletion: Is the active self a limited resource? *Journal of Personality and Social Psychology*, *74*(5), 1252–65.

Educating Amy (10 Jun. 2024). Happy mom's *[sic]*, thriving kids: How Mom's happiness fuels children's academic and emotional success. Retrieved from https://educatingamy.com/en-gb/blogs/early-child-development/the-impact-of-maternal-happiness-on-child-success.

Janssen, A. (15 Mar. 2023). How to juggle priorities: Decide which balls are glass and which are plastic. Retrieved from https://ashleyjanssen.com/how-to-juggle-priorities-decide-which-balls-are-glass-and-which-are-plastic/.

Matozzo, M. (1 Apr. 2025). Gen Z is opting for Steve Jobs-style work uniforms to avoid 'decision fatigue'. *New York Post*. Retrieved from https://nypost.com/2025/04/01/lifestyle/

gen-z-is-opting-for-steve-jobs-style-work-uniforms-to-avoid-decision-fatigue/.

Chapter 8: Routines into Rituals

Cascio, C. N., O'Donnell, M. B., Tinney, F. J., Lieberman, M. D., Taylor, S. E., Strecher, V. J. and Falk, E. B. (2016). Self-affirmation activates brain systems associated with self-related processing and reward and is reinforced by future orientation. *Social Cognitive and Affective Neuroscience*, 11(4), 621–9.

Debes, S. R. (24 Aug. 2022). How subliminal images impact your brain and behavior. Technology Networks. Retrieved from https://www.technologynetworks.com/neuroscience/articles/how-subliminal-images-impact-your-brain-and-behavior-344858.

Gallagher, K., *The Goddess Path*.

Herrmann, N. (22 December. 1997) What is the function of the various brain waves? *Scientific American*. Retrieved from: https://www.scientificamerican.com/article/what-is-the-function-of-t-1997-12-22/

Kaser, V.A. (July. 1986). The effects of an auditory subliminal message upon the production of images and dreams. *The Journal of Nervous and Mental Disease*, 174(7), 397–407.

Chapter 9: Deliberate Daydreaming

Business Sapience (20 Oct. 2023). The $10 million check Jim Carrey wrote to himself when he was unemployed [video]. YouTube. Retrieved from https://www.youtube.com/watch?v=P_Wovx6tRnY.

Grynko, S. (18 Sep. 2020). How did Oprah Winfrey manifest all her success? Medium. Retrieved from https://sebgrynko.medium.

com/how-did-oprah-winfrey-manifest-all-her-success-a76ae4bd2de.

Netflix (2023). *Arnold* [documentary]. Retrieved from https://www.netflix.com/gb/title/81317673.

Newmark, T. (2012) Cases in Visualisation for Improved Athletic Performance. *Psychiatric Annals, 42*(10), 385–387.

Pascual-Leone, A. (2001) The Brain That Plays Music and Is Changed by It. *Annals of the New York Academy of Sciences, 930*(1), 315–329.

Sharky Charts. (15 Jan. 2010.) Your words and thoughts have physical power – Will Smith [video]. YouTube. Retrieved from: https://www.youtube.com/watch?v=pfWGoLj1JCM&t=38s.

Walter, D. (23 Jan. 2022). 3 cold-calling secrets from Sara Blakely, founder of Spanx. Entrepreneur. Retrieved from https://www.entrepreneur.com/growing-a-business/3-cold-calling-secrets-from-sara-blakely-founder-of-spanx/403023.

Chapter 10: Future You

Kempton, B. (2019). *Calm Christmas and a Happy New Year: A Little Book of Festive Joy* (Piatkus).

Chapter 11: The Woman You Want to Become

Messiah, L. (2021). *Style Therapy: 30 Days to Your Signature Style* (Abrams Image).

van Elven, M. (16 Aug. 2018). People do not wear at least 50 percent of their wardrobes, says study. Fashion United. Retrieved from https://fashionunited.uk/news/fashion/people-do-not-wear-at-least-50-percent-of-their-wardrobes-according-to-study/2018081638356.

Chapter 12: Rich Mum Vibes

Costa Dias, M., Elming, W. and Joyce, R. (23 Aug. 2016). Gender wage gap grows year on year after childbirth as mothers in low-hours jobs see no wage progression. IFS. Retrieved from https://ifs.org.uk/news/gender-wage-gap-grows-year-year-after-childbirth-mothers-low-hours-jobs-see-no-wage.

Fawcett Society (22 Nov. 2023). Equal Pay Day 2023: Unlocking flexible work. Retrieved from https://www.fawcettsociety.org.uk/equal-pay-day-2023.

Fernandes, J. (10 Oct. 2024). Mukesh Ambani takes top spot on Forbes 2024 richest Indians list, Gautam Adani second – check top 10 here. Livemint. Retrieved from https://www.livemint.com/companies/news/mukesh-ambani-top-spot-forbes-2024-richest-indians-list-gautam-adani-second-top-10-jindal-damani-mittal-birla-bajaj-tata-11728546838735.html.

Frances, A. (2020). *Rich As F*ck: More Money Than You Know What to Do With* (Amanda Frances Inc.).

TUC (2021). Denied and discriminated against: The reality of flexible working for working mums. Retrieved from https://www.tuc.org.uk/sites/default/files/2021-10/Report.pdf.

Acknowledgements

This book is something I have been deeply passionate about for so long. As I look back over my years of podcasting, my intention always came back to one simple mission: how do I make this possible for women like me? Mothers.

So thank you to all the people who have led me to here. Thank you to my daughters for being my biggest teachers in life. To my eldest daughter Bohemia, for truly being my best friend during the massive changes we've lived through in the past five years, for asking me repeatedly, 'Have you written your book yet Mum?' and for choosing to go as *me* for World Book Day – iconic moves.

Thank you to the strong women in my family, from my distant ancestors whose names I don't even know, to my nan, Jean, and my mum, Cassandra. I never take for granted all they went through so that we get to live the lives we have today. Also Cass is well happy about her daughter having a book published by Penguin Random House! Bragging rights for life down at the pensioners bowling club for her!

Thank you to my sister, Anouska. If you don't have an older sister who will drive over at midnight with a pair of old, used nipple shields when you have newborns and mastitis then I feel for you – everyone needs an Anouska.

Thank you to my right-hand man who I 100 per cent manifested, my guardian angel Jay who makes work so much fun! He truly drags me and my business into 2025 on the daily.

Thank you to Mart for forcing his way into my life – it was just what I needed! You've made this journey so much fun.

Thank you to Paul Brunson for saying my name in rooms I've never been in, to Holly Whitaker at Penguin Random House and my agent Jo Bell for believing that this idea could work, and to my publicist Charlotte Tobin, you were right – I did need to write a book! And the whole team at Penguin Random House for their amazing work from incredible editing that cut out all the bits that would probably get me cancelled to a beautiful cover which was exactly what I was dreaming of.

Finally, thank you to my listeners and Book Club Bitches. You've been with me from the absolute depths of my despair to the heights of life's most amazing moments. You've cried with me, laughed with me, manifested alongside me and, honestly, you probably know me better than some people IRL. I hope that in sharing everything and baring my soul I've shown you what true manifestation and metamorphosis look like, and that they're possible for you too. Thank you for holding space for me, for showing up episode after episode and reminding me that I'm never alone on this wild ride. You've been my cheerleaders, my sounding board and my spiritual hype bitches. I love you more than words can say and, truly, this wouldn't exist without you. I've always been so passionate about sharing the law of attraction, but thanks to you I no longer have a reluctant audience of two drunk girls in the smoking area of a gay club – it's my actual, fricking *job*! I hope the journey has shown how the law of attraction has changed my life, and that it's gonna change yours too, bitches!